D1248973

Rational-Emotive Family Therapy:
A Systems Perspective

Charles H. Huber, Ph.D. is Chairperson of the Counseling and Educational Psychology Department at New Mexico State University. Previously he was Director of Psychological Services at The Samaritan Center, Jacksonville, Florida. A licensed psychologist, he is also a Clinical Member and Approved Supervisor of the American Association for Marriage and Family Therapy, and a Fellow and Approved Supervisor of the Institute for Rational-Emotive Therapy. Active in several professional organizations including the American Association for Marriage and Family Therapy, the American Psychological Association, the Association for the Advancement of Behavior Therapy, and the North American Society of Adlerian Psychology, he regularly conducts presentations and workshops within the profession and throughout communities in the United States on issues relating to marriage and the family.

Dr. Huber received his B.A. from Upsala College, his M.Ed. and Ed.S. from Florida Atlantic University, and his Ph.D. from the University of South Carolina. He completed a Post-Doctoral Fellowship at the Institute for Rational-Emotive Therapy. An editor and author, he has made numerous contributions to professional journals. He has coauthored five books with Leroy Baruth: *Coping with Marital Conflict* (1981), *An Introduction to Marital Theory and Therapy* (1984), *Counseling and Psychotherapy: Theoretical Analyses and Skills Applications* (1985), *Ethical, Legal and Professional Issues in the Practice of Marriage and Family Therapy* (1987), and *Experiencing Relationship Enhancement* (1987).

Leroy G. Baruth, Ed.D. is Professor and Chair, Department of Human Development and Psychological Counseling at the Appalachian State University, North Carolina. A licensed counseling psychologist, he is also an Approved Supervisor of the American Association for Marriage and Family Therapy. Active in the American Association for Marriage and Family Therapy, the American Association for Counseling and Development, and the American Psychological Association, Dr. Baruth has received a number of awards from these and other organizations. He has served as a consultant to college and university personnel, social service agencies, and private and public school systems. He regularly presents at state, regional, and national professional association conventions.

Dr. Baruth obtained his B.S. and M.S. from Mankato State University and his Ed.D. from the University of Arizona. His numerous articles on various aspects of counseling and psychotherapy have appeared in a wide range of professional journals. He has authored or coauthored twelve books, including *A Single Parent's Survival Guide* (1979), *Child Psychology* with Alaine Lane (1980), and *The ABC's of Classroom Discipline* with Dan G. Eckstein (1982).

616.89156
H86

Rational-Emotive Family Therapy

A Systems Perspective

Charles H. Huber, Ph.D.
Leroy G. Baruth, Ed.D.

SPRINGER PUBLISHING COMPANY
New York

82364

Copyright © 1989 by Springer Publishing Company, Inc.
All rights reserved.

No part of this publication may be reproduced, stored in a retrieval
system, or transmitted in any form or by any means, electronic,
mechanical, photocopying, recording, or otherwise, without the prior
permission of Springer Publishing Company, Inc.

Springer Publishing Company, Inc.
536 Broadway
New York, NY 10012

89 90 91 92 93 / 5 4 3 2 1

Library of Congress Cataloging-in-Publication Data

Huber, Charles H., 1949–
  Rational-emotive family therapy : a systems perspective / Charles
H. Huber, Leroy G. Baruth.
    p.   cm.
  Bibliography: p.
  Includes index.
  ISBN 0-8261-6100-6
  1. Family psychotherapy. 2. Rational-emotive psychotherapy.
I. Baruth, Leroy G. II. Title.
RC488.5.H824 1989
616.89′156—dc19   88-39901
                                                               CIP

Printed in the United States of America

#18624796

Contents

Foreword

During the 60s and 70s traditional psychotherapeutic approaches were confronted with an extraordinary number of assaults from a wide range of theorists and practitioners leaving psychotherapy in a total state of confusion. More importantly this state of confusion forced the practicing psychotherapists to join forces with one or another approach and to remain "faithful" or "congruent" to their chosen theoretical approach. Fortunately, during the 80s a growing trend toward integration has developed; there is even a growing agreement that cognitive-behavioral approaches to change are more effective than less structured or passive approaches. At the same time family therapy has become increasingly popular, as psychotherapists are sought to help families function more effectively in a rapidly changing society where traditional values are questioned.

With the growing popularity of systemic approaches, many psychotherapists have incorporated the techniques and strategies advocated by systems theorists without truly having a focus for change. What are we really changing when we manipulate family interactions to change family dynamics? Emphasis is placed on implementing a process which is theorized to bring about a change in family members and in the system as a whole. Many of these approaches lack philosophical understanding or explanation of human behavior.

Huber and Baruth close the gap between theory and practice. In this book they provide a solid theoretical foundation for Rational-Emotive Family Therapy. Their merging of cybernetics and Rational-Emotive Therapy is carefully conceptualized and remains faithful to both. The organization of the book into three parts (1) Theoretical Foundations, (2) Therapeutic Implications, and (3) Clinical Applications offers the reader a solid understanding of the integration, as well as a clear model for implementation. Chapters 5 and 6 clearly organize for the family therapist an approach and directionality currently lacking in many family-therapy approaches. They also provide the Rational-Emotive Therapist with an approach which is philosophically consistent with their individual and group therapy techniques.

The focus on changing attitudes and beliefs of family members is unquestionably a step in the right direction. Huber and Baruth's approach helps family members discover and change family "rules" that are at the core of dysfunctional families. Their creative interventions outlined in Chapter 6 will be a welcome addition to any therapists' repertoire of behavior. The verbatim case studies in Chapters 7 and 8 provide the reader with an excellent model and beginning point to practice Rational-Emotive Family Therapy.

In the preface the authors state: ". . . there has been no seminal book length work to offer the novice or experienced practitioner a comprehensive presentation. This book has been prepared to fill this serious void given the popularity of Rational-Emotive Therapy and the systemic family therapy perspective." They have achieved their goal. Undoubtedly this book will be the first of many integrating two major trends in psychotherapy; cognitive-behavioral and family systems. It could easily become a pioneering volume for the 90s.

Dominic J. DiMattia, Ed.D.
Senior Staff Supervisor and
Director of Corporate Services,
Institute for Rational-Emotive
Therapy; Virginia & Harvey
Hubbell Professor of Counseling,
University of Bridgeport

Preface

Over the past three decades, Rational-Emotive Therapy (RET) has become one of the most influential forms of psychotherapy. It is practiced by literally thousands of mental health professionals throughout the world. The enormous impact of Rational-Emotive Therapy and its founder, Dr. Albert Ellis, on these practitioners has been identified consistently in the professional literature. For example, Smith (1982) reported Ellis was ranked second only to Carl Rogers and ahead of Sigmund Freud by over 800 clinical and counseling psychologists asked whom they considered the most influential contributor to the field of psychotherapy. Smith also noted that rational and/or cognitive behavioral therapy was the predominant representation among the ten most influential contributors cited.

The same three decades which have experienced the emergence of Rational-Emotive Therapy have also encompassed a concomitant increase in the number of mental health professionals embracing a systemic family therapy perspective: An emphasis focusing therapeutic efforts on the family system rather than on individual family members or an individual client. While this perspective finds meaning in the symptoms exhibited by the individual, these manifestations are viewed as covariate aspects of family relationships. Consequently, the "client" for family therapists is the family system including the individual rather than the individual in isolation; interventions target improvement in the overall family functioning or in specific intrafamily relationships as well as individual member's symptoms.

While Ellis and other Rational-Emotive writers have addressed the interface between Rational-Emotive Therapy and the systemic family therapy perspective in brief writings (e.g., Ellis, 1982; Woullf, 1983), there unfortunately has been no seminal book length work to offer the novice nor experienced practitioner a comprehensive presentation. This book has been prepared to fill this serious void given the popularity of Rational-Emotive Therapy and the systemic family therapy perspective.

Rational-Emotive Family Therapy: A Systems Perspective is structured to detail the essentials of this powerful therapeutic interface. The book is divided into three major parts. Part I addresses the theoretical foundations of Rational-Emotive Family Therapy (REFT). Chapter 1 contains an overview of the family systems perspective with special emphasis apportioned to the understandings afforded by cybernetics within that larger perspective. Chapter 2 considers the major components of the Rational-Emotive position. Chapter 3 acknowledges the simultaneous communications offered by the Rational-Emotive position and family systems perspective. It offers the concept of "the meaningful new" represented here by the Mental Research Institute strategy, a theory of change that equally and conceptually complements both RET and family systems perspectives. The evolving cybernetic system therein is REFT.

Part II posits the therapeutic implications of REFT. Chapter 4 delineates therapist distinctions, those guidelines that set the stage and organize the clinical practice of REFT. Chapter 5 outlines the assessment portions of REFT therapeutic efforts. Chapter 6 continues these efforts with strategic change processes. Part III offers selected clinical applications of REFT. Chapters 7 and 8 provide case studies illustrating how REFT comes to life in actual practice, while Chapter 9 looks at training and supervision in REFT. These final three chapters all include verbatim transcriptions of sessions, the first two clinical and the latter, supervisory.

Rational-Emotive Family Therapy:
A Systems Perspective

Part I

Theoretical Foundations

There is an enormous difference between an academic understanding of systems and an actual reorganization of one's thinking so that families are experienced as systems.

1

The Family-Systems Perspective

The development of family therapy as a primary therapeutic approach has been based on much more than the discovery of a new method and an enlarged social unit of treatment. It is the product of a new epistemology, a new way of conceptualizing the nature of the mind and about the determinants of behavior (Hoffman, 1981). In the beginning days of family therapy, clinicians were primarily concerned with defending clients against the influence of their families. Schizophrenic patients, for example, were viewed as the victims of double-binding parents and schizophrenogenic mothers. However, further observation led to a profound shift away from this formulation of patients versus parents (Nichols, 1984).

Eventually all family members came to be viewed as victims; the whole family needed to be changed. The family was no longer seen as simply an aggregate of individuals, but as a system. This conceptualization is the central, yet most frequently misunderstood idea in family therapy. There is an enormous difference between an academic understanding of systems and an actual reorganization of one's thinking so that families are *experienced* as systems. Seeing people only as independent individuals is frequently an extremely difficult habit to transcend. The discussion that follows serves as an introduction to acquiring a family-systems perspective.

GENERAL SYSTEMS THEORY

The individual is a part, not a whole. This seemingly innocuous statement, implies a huge step away from former conventional philosophical

3

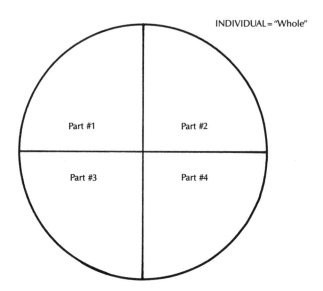

FIGURE 1.1   Nonsystemic psychology views the individual as a whole consisting of parts.

Adapted from: S. J. Schultz, *Family Systems Therapy: An Integration* (New York: Jason Aronson, 1984). Copyright 1984 by Jason Aronson. Reprinted by permission of the publisher.

and scientific thinking. The individual person has traditionally been the subject matter of psychology. Conventional, nonsystemic psychology views the individual as a *whole consisting of parts* (Figure 1.1). It explains the behavior of the whole (the person) in terms of its constituent parts. For example, in psychodynamic psychology, the parts might be the id, ego, and superego. In biological psychology, the parts would include the various nervous and glandular functions.

By contrast, systems theory views the individual person as *part of a larger whole* rather than a whole in itself (Figure 1.2). The behavior of the part (the person) is explained in terms of its relationship with the other parts and its function for the whole. For example, to understand the behavior of an acting-out child, a systems perspective would advocate not only looking within the child, but taking a further look at the child as part of the family system, perhaps wondering about the child's role in sidetracking the parents' marital conflict.

This apparently small shift in perspective in viewing the individual as a part rather than as a whole has profound consequences. In taking this perspective, cherished philosophical and scientific points of view

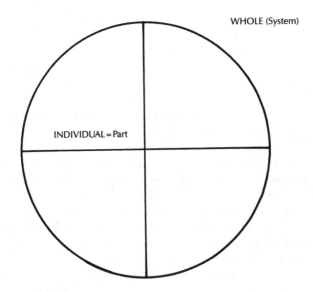

FIGURE 1.2   According to systems theory, the individual person is part of a larger whole (system).

Adapted from: S. J. Schultz, *Family Systems Therapy: An Integration* (New York: Jason Aronson, 1984). Copyright 1984 by Jason Aronson. Reprinted by permission of the publisher.

as well as a common belief about what family therapy is about must be departed from.

The primacy and responsibility of the individual is so much a part of Western thought that it is difficult to even consider thinking another way. Modifying notions about the value of personal autonomy, "being the captain of one's soul," internal motivation and the like represent significant perceptual shifts. Acquiring a systemic perspective also calls for a departure from traditional Western scientific explanation (Schultz, 1984).

Since at least the time of Aristotle, the nature of scientific explanation has been debated. With the rise of classical physics in the 17th century, however, one type of explanation supplanted the rest and became established as the preeminent form of scientific understanding. Referred to as a *mechanical* explanation, this nonsystemic form of scientific understanding results in a general goal of reducing reality into ever-smaller units in order to determine the cause of individual events. Rules or laws governing the elementary parts are sought in order to then understand larger complex phenomena. This mechanical explanation has been characterized as "the whole is nothing more than the sum of its parts" (Beavers, 1977, p. 11) and was illustrated earlier in Figure 1.1.

According to a mechanical explanation, everything in the physical world is governed by the inexorable laws of linear causality. The most relevant example of this linear thinking is the stimulus–response theory in psychology. A leads to B, B leads to C, C leads to D in a chain of linear causality. Linear thinking has some definite and demonstrable advantages. By relying on a series of linear cause-and-effect occurrences, one can predict outcomes by linking such sequences. Likewise, one can start with an event and work backward until a basic cause is discovered. This perspective, however, leaves some things unexplained. Life phenomena (living things) do not necessarily yield easily to study under the mechanical explanation of the physical sciences (Rapoport, 1968). Often, much of the phenomena being studied has to be left out of consideration in order to predict outcomes or find beginning causes (Steinglass, 1978).

The eminent biologist Ludwig von Bertalanffy, who published the concept of General Systems Theory in 1945, believed that an alternative model of explanation was needed for the life sciences. General Systems Theory was developed to go beyond mechanistic physics to include the interfunctioning of parts that make up whole systems, and beyond static concepts to take account of the temporal quality of life and the omnipresence of change (Nichols, 1984). The development of General Systems Theory saw a focus on organization rather than reductionism. Organizing principles or relationships that result when the entire entity is taken into consideration are emphasized. Behavior, including growth and creativity, can be considered and accounted for by the dynamic interaction among the components of a living system.

In essence, "the whole is different from the sum of its parts" characterizes the General Systems Theory perspective. That is, when the parts are examined separately, the findings cannot simply be added together in order to determine what the whole will look like. The whole must be examined as a whole, as a system, rather than as simply the sum of a number of parts (Nichols & Everett, 1986).

CYBERNETICS AND CIRCULAR CAUSALITY

Confusion is often expressed relative to the relationship between General Systems Theory and cybernetics. Although the two are at times equated, they are not the same. General Systems Theory is the broader

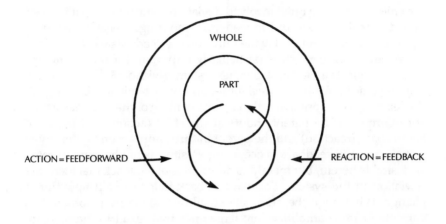

FIGURE 1.3 The basic cybernetic model. A closed informational loop consisting of some action of the part on the whole (feedforward portion of the loop) plus a reaction of the whole back on the part (feedback portion of the loop).

Adapted from: S. J. Schultz, *Family Systems Therapy: An Integration* (New York: Jason Aronson, 1984). Copyright 1984 by Jason Aronson. Reprinted by permission of the publisher.

of the two conceptualizations, referring to all self-regulating systems, of which the cybernetic model is one type (Nichols, 1984).

Cybernetics essentially has to do with how systems are regulated, that is, how they remain stable or change. In the cybernetic model, part and whole are linked by a closed informational loop (Figure 1.3). The part performs some action (e.g., a person engages in a specific behavior) that has an impact on the whole. This is the *feedforward* part of the loop. The whole then has some reaction back upon the part. This is the *feedback* portion of the loop. This relationship between the action and reaction portions of the informational loop has been categorized as of two types: negative or deviation-reducing feedback and positive or deviation-amplifying feedback (Schultz, 1984).

In the case of negative or deviation-reducing feedback, the reaction to the original action results in less of that original action. For example, if a parent was to shout at a child (action) and the child then became quiet, giving in to placate the parent's outburst (reaction), and the parent then quieted down (less of the original action), negative feedback has restored their system to its original tranquil state. It is important to note that the deviation reduction is a property of the feedback loop as a whole, not of any part of it alone. It would not be possible to say that the child's becoming quiet involved deviation reduction until it is ascertained that the parent did indeed stop shouting. Negative feedback helps explain how things stay the same, how a steady state is maintained in systems. This concept is particularly important for family therapy relative to efforts aimed at stabilizing systems (Nichols & Everett, 1986).

In the case of positive or deviation-amplifying feedback, by contrast, the reaction to the original action results in more of that original action. For example, if the parent shouts at the child (action) and the child shouts back (reaction) and the parent in turn shouts even louder (more action), positive feedback is occurring. Positive is not to be interpreted as desirable herein, but merely as descriptive of feedback that increases deviation in the system. Positive feedback helps explain how things change. What might be originally small deviations from some initial condition can be amplified into large ones that result in the reorganization of the system or, in some cases, threaten its integrity. Positive feedback is particularly relevant in family therapy wherein efforts are aimed at changing patterns of relating and behaving or breaking up an existing system (Nichols & Everett, 1986).

Just as General Systems Theory reshapes conventional Western notions of scientific explanation, so does cybernetics because it introduces the idea of circular causality by way of the feedback loop. Linear causality suggests that event A causes event B. Circular causality, by contrast, proposes that any delineation of before and after, or cause and effect, is purely arbitrary. Instead, behavior is viewed as a series of moves and countermoves in a repeating cycle. A teenage daughter may be convinced that her mother's nagging (cause) makes her withdraw. The mother may be equally convinced that the daughter's withdrawal causes her to nag. From a systems perspective, however, their behavior would be seen as part of a circular pattern: the more the mother nags, the more the daughter withdraws and the more the daughter withdraws, the more the mother nags. Who started the sequence is not considered relevant for resolving the problem because once underway, these sequences seem to be self-perpetuating.

The participants in such a sequence typically find themselves trapped in the epistemology of a linear model of causality. Each thinks, "If only I try harder (more nagging, or more withdrawal) I can make the other change." Change, unfortunately, rarely occurs because in trying to change the dysfunctional pattern, participants tend to continue acting it out, only more forcefully. Even when blaming ("Mother's nagging makes me withdraw") is replaced by confessions of guilt ("Maybe my withdrawal makes her nag") the illusion of linear causality is maintained. From a cybernetic viewpoint, both the mother and daughter are inferring linear causality in what is more a mutual causal process and thus they lack a viewpoint from which to adaptively alter it.

SIMPLE CYBERNETICS

The basic elements of a cybernetic system are a receptor, an analyzer, and an effector connected by a closed feedback loop (Figure 1.4). The receptor receives information from the environment and transmits it to the analyzer. The analyzer processes this input and arrives at a decision forwarding it to the effector. The effector translates the analyzer's decision into an output action upon the environment. The feedback loop (illustrated in Figure 1.4 by the arrow to the left, from the effector through the environment and back to the receptor) provides the receptor with information about the effect of the system's action upon the environment.

The common thermostatic system for controlling room temperature is a familiar example of a cybernetic system. The system includes a thermometer (the receptor), the thermostat (the analyzer), and the furnace (the effector). The environment in this case is the rest of the world, in particular, a room, apartment, or house. In this everyday model of simple cybernetics, the analyzer is preset for a certain value, the desired temperature, by a human operator who is outside the system under consideration. As long as the temperature is below the desired value, the information forwarded to the thermostat (analyzer) by the thermometer (receptor) leads the thermostat to conclude "too cold" and a message is sent to the furnace (effector) requesting "more heat." The thermostatic system utilizes a negative feedback loop to reduce deviation from the desired temperature, here warming up the room because it has become too cold.

Eventually the temperature reaches the desired value. Now the information sent from the thermometer to the thermostat leads the thermostat to conclude "too hot" and a message is forwarded to the furnace to "shut down." Again, the negative feedback loop reduces deviation from the preset temperature, this time resulting in the furnace being turned off to keep the room from becoming hotter still.

A plausible, although unlikely example of a cybernetic system wherein a positive feedback loop results in deviation amplification as opposed to deviation reduction was offered by Schultz (1984). He described a married couple who got the dual controls of their electric blanket crossed.

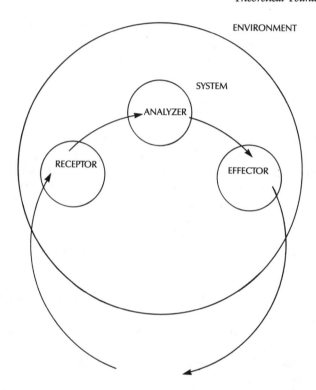

FIGURE 1.4 A cybernetic system, here consisting of three subsystems (receptor, analyzer, and effector) connected by a closed informational loop.

Adapted from: S. J. Schultz, *Family Systems Therapy: An Integration* (New York: Jason Aronson, 1984). Copyright 1984 by Jason Aronson. Reprinted by permission of the publisher.

The husband became too hot and turned down "his" control. Since he actually turned down the temperature on his wife's side of the blanket, he remained too hot and turned down "his" control some more. Eventually, his wife became uncomfortably cold and turned up "her" control, heating up her husband's side of the blanket even more, leading him to turn "his" control down further. Figure 1.5 illustrates this as a cybernetic conceptualization (the husband being arbitrarily made part of the system while his wife is made part of the environment).

DISTINCTION AND RECURSIVE COMPLEMENTARITY

Although essential to acquiring a family-systems perspective, an understanding of negative or deviation-reducing and positive or deviation-

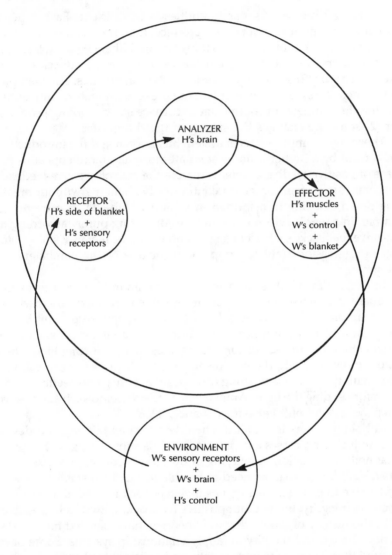

FIGURE 1.5 An illustration of deviation-amplifying feedback. The couple (H, Husband; W, Wife) get the dual controls of their electric blanket crossed.

Adapted from: S. J. Schultz, *Family Systems Therapy: An Integration* (New York: Jason Aronson, 1984). Copyright 1984 by Jason Aronson. Reprinted by permission of the publisher.

amplifying systems as separate entities is insufficient. Each type of system will continue to work (i.e., produce unending sameness or continuous change) until one of two things occur. Either (1) the system fails (some component of the system breaks down or a feedback loop is disrupted); or (2) some higher order system intervenes. For example, a thermostatic system will maintain the preset temperature until either (1) the thermometer or thermostat or furnace stops working properly, or (2) someone changes the setting of the thermostat.

These twin complications of system breakdown and the introduction of control by a higher-order system are normally more critical in the case of positive-feedback systems than in the case of negative-feedback systems. No system can go on continuously changing without breaking down or being transformed in some way. To cite an extreme example, in a war between two countries operating purely according to positive feedback, each act of aggression would be met by a still greater act of aggression until the population of one of the combatants is eliminated.

In the realm of physical aggression, common occurrences in the animal world illustrate how systems are able to maintain themselves. For example, in fights to establish dominance, aggression builds to a point at which the physical superiority of one of the combatants is established. But instead of continuing to escalate to further bloodshed and ultimately death, the vanquished animal displays signs of submission with the system switching from positive to negative feedback and therefore ending the fight. Animal behaviorists refer to such submissive displays as "cut-off" behavior (Chance, 1966).

Pathology occurs in families when deviation-amplifying and deviation-reducing processes are imbalanced. This should suggest, however, that neither deviation-amplifying or deviation-reducing processes are "bad." All living systems need to be able to maintain stability as well as be able to change. Clearly, negative feedback is needed to insure a system's integrity, but without positive feedback, growth is impossible.

In the history of family therapy, theorists have debated how to describe change and stability in family-relationship systems. Some have argued that families are homeostatic and resistant to change. At other times, families have been described as perpetual processes of change which are evolutionary in nature. This dichotomy of positions suggests that experience is best structured in terms of pairs, dualities, or distinctions. By contrast, Slater (1974) asserted that "any pattern, value, ideal, or behavioral tendency is always present at any time, along with its polar opposite. Only the relative emphasis given each pole and the ways of arranging their simultaneous expression tend to change" (pp. 182–183).

Keeney and Ross (1985) proposed that family therapy may be viewed in such a fashion: "a particular communication can be seen as half of a more encompassing pair, duality, or distinction" (p. 47). Consider the following family scenario:

Roles within the C family were established early and remained more or less fixed thereafter. When David was born, he became Mrs. C's responsibility. Tired at night, lonely, and bored with her husband working long hours and/or socializing with his friends, Mrs. C became increasingly resentful of being neglected by Mr. C In turn, her progressive refusal of his sexual advances infuriated him, to which he responded by withdrawing into work and friends even further. A stalemate resulted with Mr. C staying away from home more and more and Mrs. C developing a closer and closer relationship with David, whom she began to interact with as a substitute for her husband. As he grew up, David had few friends and was considered a "mama's boy." Ashamed of the nonexistent relationship between his parents, he never invited a friend to his home. His schoolmates have come to think of David, now 15, as increasingly odd, a loner. He, too, has come to see himself similarly, as have his parents.

One implication that can be made from this brief overview of the C family is that David's "symptomology" serves to protect his parents from having to address their marital dissatisfaction. Were a request made for David to become more age-appropriately peer-oriented, this might also be seen as representing a simultaneous although possibly unstated request to the parents to change their behavior. Stated in a different way, any proposal to change symptomatic experience also implies a request to change the way in which stability is maintained in the family.

In general no distinction can be made without making a multiple communication. Change cannot be spoken of without implying stability. Similarly one cannot speak of competition without cooperation, parts without wholes, and so on. Whenever a differention is made, two ways of talking about its sides are always present: (1) their *distinction* may be addressed; or (2) their *connection* may be addressed (Keeney & Ross, 1985). Returning to the above illustration of the C family, one might choose to see David's parents as requesting he change without any consideration for how that change connects with the stability of their marital relationship. Or one may choose to see the complementary connection of change and stability.

As an example of distinction–connection apart from the realm of family therapy, Keeney and Ross (1985) proposed a consideration of the distinction in the animal world between predator (foxes) and prey (rabbits). They described the logic of this relationship as being specified in terms of the fox attempting to catch the rabbit where there can be victory only for the fox (unless the absence of a victory by the fox is viewed as victory for the rabbit). Utilizing the level of individual rabbits and foxes, the fox would be seen as achieving a victory. On the level of species interaction, however, the population size of the fox will be directly related to the population size of rabbits. Each individual victory for a fox may ultimately contribute to a loss for the overall fox population.

Any distinction cast in terms of victories and losses alone is incomplete. For the predator/prey dichotomy, a more encompassing system frames it; that being the ecosystem/species interaction. The patterns of species interaction provide the way in which an entire ecosystem is kept in balance. To take the side of either predator or prey is to risk disrupting a larger pattern of interaction. Thus, a distinction with an underlying logic of competition is also part of a more encompassing distinction with an underlying logic of cooperation (Varela, 1979). Predator/prey points to a logic of competition, whereas ecosystem/ species interaction points to a logic of cooperation. To be asked the question, "What is the relationship between foxes and rabbits?" within this perspective would best be clarified with the question, "At what level? They battle with each other as individual members, but cooperate with each other as whole species."

In family therapy requests presented by a family to unilaterally change one of its member's symptomatic experience underscore the distinction between who has the problem; who is the patient and who is not? From the aforementioned perspective incorporating a higher order view the family can be seen as cooperating on a more encompassing level in such a way that each member contributes to the stability of the relationship structure.

All distinctions in family therapy can therefore be seen as either: (1) a duality of excluding opposites; or (2) a recursive complementarity of self-referential sides. "Recursive complementarity refers to the higher-order view where the interaction between different sides is underscored . . . the two sides must maintain a difference to interact, while their interaction connects them as a whole system" (Keeney & Ross, 1985, pp. 48–49). Recursive complementarity explains how different sides of a relationship participate as a complementary connection and yet remain distinct.

Varela (1979) proposed that any distinction taken as an either/or duality can be reframed as the right-hand side of a more encompassing recursive complementarity. Making this perceptual shift, what might have once appeared to be battling opposites becomes a pattern of interaction stabilizing the organization of a whole system. For family therapy, the duality of excluding opposites would result in the absence or presence of symptomatic experience, most likely in one family member. Recursive complementarity, by contrast, would underscore a view of each family member contributing to the stabilization of the whole family system as it presently finds itself, symptomatic or otherwise.

CYBERNETICS OF CYBERNETICS

In the development of simple cybernetics, reference was frequently made to the study of "black boxes." This study was generally restricted to examining the relationship of what went into a system (input) and what came out of it (output). The relationship was cybernetic when the output was viewed as acting upon the input so as to modify future output. For example, in a cybernetic system regulating room temperature in a home, the thermostatic system regulates itself by recycling information about the present room temperature in order to determine its future operations. The shortcoming of this simple cybernetic perspective, however, is that it fails to include the human being who is necessary to calibrate the preset temperature by adjusting the setting on the thermostat. In general, any "black box" system such as a simple heating system, is circumscribed by a higher order of feedback control (Keeney, 1983).

The black-box perspective which posits an observer outside the phenomena being observed often leads to the idea that the outsider is in a position to unilaterally manipulate or control the system. Early family therapy efforts emanating from this view had as a goal "generating a correct intervention" that would eradicate the presenting symptomatic problem. Keeney and Ross (1983) described this as family therapy's "Primitive Period":

> This unilineal view brings to mind the image of a primitive man with a spear in his hand. From his perspective, the art of therapy involved positioning oneself at an appropriate distance from which the target of intervention could be clearly discerned. The therapist's job was then analogous

to choosing a spear of correct weight and design that could be successfully hurled toward the target. (p. 375)

This Primitive Period perspective has been a valuable one. Well-defined distinctions between therapist, intervention, and target problem facilitate a simple cybernetic conceptualization of the therapeutic process. The family has been depicted as a black-box system which can be acted upon by an outside therapist. Within this conceptualization, the effects of the therapist's interventions on the family system are able to be utilized to alter, correct, and shape subsequent interventions. This perspective is also sometimes useful when one is given the responsibility for managing a system. For example, the caseworker who is instructed by a court system to supervise the family where child abuse has been chronic will be grateful for a black box view. This view enables the caseworker to discern patterns that maintain the problem behaviors as well as orient specific intervention strategies.

Historically, the black-box view of simple cybernetics came to be associated with technical, theoretical, and biological limitations. Howe and von Foerster (1974) suggested that "while cybernetics began by developing the epistemology for comprehending and simulating first-order regulatory processes in the animal and machine, cybernetics today provides a conceptual framework with sufficient richness to attack successfully second-order process" (p. 16).

The most relevant consequence of this higher order cybernetic view proposed by Howe and von Foerster involves how the position of the therapist in family therapy is seen. While early family therapy efforts saw the family system as a black box that could be observed and operated on from an outside position, their view brings the therapist into the system, prohibiting any disconnection of the therapist–family circuit. The movement from black box to black box *plus* observer represents an evolution from simple cybernetics to "cybernetics of cybernetics," a phrase originally suggested by Margaret Mead (1968) to point out the observer's inclusion and participation in the system. As von Foerster (1973) concluded, "It is at this point where we mature from cybernetics (where the observer enters the system only by stipulating its purpose) to cybernetics of cybernetics (where the observer enters the system by stipulating his own purpose)" (p. 31).

To return to the earlier image of "primitive" family therapy, from the perspective of simple cybernetics, a therapist would deliver an intervention from an outside position and then, from that outside position, observe the effects of the intervention to modify subsequent interventions. With cybernetics of cybernetics, a higher order view is generated. When the therapist throws the spear, so to speak, that therapist remains connected to the spear and travels with it. Consequently, the therapist as observer and spear thrower becomes part of what is being treated, observed, and thrown (Keeney & Ross, 1985).

With this higher order view, distinctions that have led to significant discussion and debate within the field of family therapy have been re-examined. These differences have included issues such as whether families experience primarily discontinuous or continuous processes of change, whether therapy is primarily an art or craft and so on. While some within the field have framed these distinctions as two sides of an either/or dichotomy, cybernetics of cybernetics offers an alternative frame of reference. Rather than proposing each side as related through a logic of negation (e.g., A/not A), it posits a logic of complementarity.

The value of this complementary framing of distinctions can be seen in the description of a "poly-ocular view" described by de Shazer (1985):

> Bateson (1979) described ideas as developing from having two or more descriptions of the same process, pattern, system, or sequence that are coded or collected differently. A bonus—the idea—develops out of the differences between or among descriptions. Metaphorically, this process is similar to that of depth perception. The right eye sees things in its way, while simultaneously the left eye sees things differently. The difference between the two eyes' views leads to the bonus of depth perception. Clearly, it is not that the right eye is correct while the left eye is wrong or visa versa. (pp. 19–20)

Extending this metaphor, it can be assumed that fusing each side of a conceptual distinction will produce a bonus, that being a higher order view.

The historical debate among family therapy theorists relative to describing change and stability in family relationships was earlier alluded to as tending to be an either/or dichotomy between arguing that families are homeostatic and resistant to change on one hand versus the view that they are in perpetual processes of change that are evolutionary in nature. The higher order view that a poly-ocular perspective provides would assert that families cannot be described as changing without consideration of their stability and vice versa. For example, the tightrope walker must continually change body position to maintain stability on the high wire. Likewise, families must change to maintain stability or, seen from the other direction, remain stable in order to change. Recognizing this complementarity requires a poly-ocular view

Cybernetic System + (Stability/Change)

FIGURE 1.6   An illustration of a cybernetic system being defined as a system which encompasses a recursive, complementary relation between processes of stability and change.

Adapted from: B. P. Keeney and J. M. Ross, *Mind in Therapy: Constructing Systemic Family Therapies* (New York: Basic Books, 1985). Copyright 1985 by Basic Books. Reprinted by permission of the publisher.

wherein change and stability are brought together through the conceptual lens of cybernetics (Keeney & Ross, 1985).

SIMULTANEOUS COMMUNICATIONS

Cybernetics has been conceptualized by Keeney and Ross (1985) as "the study of a particular recursive complementarity concerned with the interrelation of stability and change" (p. 50). This conceptualization of cybernetics is exemplified by an earlier statement by Bateson (1971, p. 381): "all changes can be understood as the effort to maintain some constancy and all constancy as maintained through change." Watzlawick, Weakland, and Fisch (1974) also alluded to this complementarity between stability and change, referring to it as "the paradoxical relationship between persistence and change" (p. 1). This interrelation is illustrated in Figure 1.6.

This recursive complementarity between stability and change specifies a cybernetic system; cybernetic systems being patterns of organization that maintain stability through processes of change. A family, when defined as a cybernetic system, is therefore a social organism whose whole pattern of organization is stabilized through the change of its component parts (Keeney & Ross, 1983).

The communications that emanate from a family defined as a cybernetic system are simultaneous. In a therapeutic setting, the troubled family might be depicted as communicating simultaneous messages requesting stability of the system *and* change in the particular way it maintains that stability. One way of summarizing this simultaneous communication is that the higher level message involves "change of change." This can be graphically illustrated as in Figure 1.7. As seen in Figure 1.7, the family system at time 2 is more adaptive than it was at time 1. In effect, the system seeks a way of changing how it changes

FIGURE 1.7   An illustration of the goal of family therapy; that being to alter the way in which a family maintains its organization through processes of change. Therapeutic intervention facilitates a more adaptive pattern of organization where the system at time 2 is more adaptive than it was at time 1.

Adapted from: B. P. Keeney and J. M. Ross, *Mind in Therapy: Constructing Systemic Family Therapies* (New York: Basic Books, 1985). Copyright 1985 by Basic Books. Reprinted by permission of the publisher.

in order to stabilize its organization as a more adaptive system (Keeney & Ross, 1985).

Following from the work of Ashby (1956) and Bateson (1979), Keeney and Ross (1985) assert that all adaptive change requires a source of the "new" from which alternative behaviors, choices, patterns, and structures may be drawn. While Ashby and Bateson referred to this source of the new as "random," Keeney and Ross identify the important realization that not all sources of randomness are change inducing. There must be a *belief* that the "new" is not only new, but also has *meaning*. Keeney and Ross referred to this as "meaningful noise." The present authors, however, find the descriptor "noise" to carry a distracting connotation and therefore refer to this source of the new as "the meaningful new."

The meaningful new is a message selectively focused on by an observing system. What is meaningful arises from the perception of the observer. If a family member believes there is meaning in a message, his or her expectation of meaning will help construct it. Sources of the meaningful new in a therapeutic setting might include references to family history, cultural myth, psychobabble, religious metaphor, anecdotes, etc. Those descriptions and explanations of themselves that family members offer will provide the focus for what form of the meaningful new will be most readily recognized.

At this point, a more complete change of change model can be illustrated as in Figure 1.8: This illustration identifies the emergence of a more adaptive pattern of organization pointed to by the meaningful new, thus representing a higher order process of change. At this higher level, the cybernetic system simultaneously requests both a change of change and a new way of stabilizing its stability. To achieve this requires a third simultaneous communication: the meaningful new.

FIGURE 1.8   Effective family therapy is here illustrated as a "change of change"
wherein the system recalibrates the way it changes in order to
remain stable by encountering a form of "meaningful new"; the
more adaptive system at time 1 pointed to by the meaningful new.

Adapted from: B. P. Keeney and J. M. Ross, *Mind in Therapy: Constructing Systemic Family
Therapies* (New York: Basic Books, 1985). Copyright 1985 by Basic Books. Reprinted by
permission of the publisher.

Successful therapy from a family-systems perspective can thus be
described as the creation of a context wherein a family system is enabled
to calibrate the way it changes in order to remain stable (Keeney & Ross,
1983). This "change of change" requires effectively addressing processes
of change and stability as well as assisting the troubled family system
encountering some meaningful new. The building and nurturance of
such contexts utilizing the Rational-Emotive position will be the subject of the upcoming chapters.

2

The Rational-Emotive Position

The Rational-Emotive position has evolved over the past three decades largely through the leadership and creative efforts of Albert Ellis (1957, 1958, 1962, 1970, 1971, 1973, 1977, 1980, 1984, 1987). The major catalyst for this evolutionary posture has been Ellis' repeatedly expressed concern that for a therapeutic position to prove ultimately effective, clients must not only begin to think, feel, and act better, but equally importantly, *continue* to do so in ways that maximize specific goal attainment as well as general life satisfaction. In his own words:

> My main goals in treating any of my psychotherapy clients are simple and concrete: to leave the client, at the end of the psychotherapeutic process, with a minimum of anxiety (or self-blame) and of hostility (or blame of others and the world around him) and just as importantly, to give him a method of self-observations and self-assessment that will insure that, for the rest of his life, he will be minimally anxious and hostile. (Ellis, 1973, p. 147)

The Rational-Emotive position derives from multiple philosophic and behavioral science theories (for reviews, see Ellis, 1962, 1973; Dolliver, 1979). What follows in this chapter represents the critical concepts and assumptions that continue to influence its development, particularly its foundation as a systemic family therapy.

THE HUMAN IMAGE

The Rational-Emotive position holds that humans are born with strong biological predispositions, including the powerful tendency to have

21

sex–love relationships and to live in some kind of family group. Following, they also have a strong tendency to be teachable and to easily learn from birth onward the customs and traditions of significant others with whom they live, particularly the members of their family of origin (Ellis, 1982). The Rational-Emotive position posits that humans are by nature fallible; perfection is an unattainable ideal. Being fallible, humans have a natural tendency to make errors and defeat themselves in the pursuit of their basic goals and purposes.

Humans are regarded as complex organisms. They have innumerable facets which comprise their total being. They are constantly in a process of flux as opposed to a static state. In spite of the fact that humans are significantly influenced by hereditary predispostions and environmental conditions that are beyond anyone's full control, they possess a good degree of potential self-determination. Whether they are consciously aware of it or not, to some extent, they choose whether or not to listen to and be further influenced by what they are born with and by what they learn. As they advance in age, they develop even greater abilities to make choices in how they function. Consequently, there is the potential to effect changes in virtually all forms of human affective, behavioral, and cognitive functioning (Ellis, 1982).

The Rational-Emotive position advances the proposition that knowledge is influenced largely by the personal evaluations humans impose on their own perceptions. Ellis has frequently placed this "constructivist" view in a historical perspective by citing Epictetus, the Roman stoic philosopher, who in the first century A.D. wrote that "humans are disturbed not by things but by the views they take of them." Knowledge then is not considered to exist in any absolute or final form.

Finally, erroneous conclusions persons take on about their world are emphasized as the primary contributions to human dysfunction. Ellis has postulated both biological and hereditary bases for this propensity toward faulty thinking processes:

> I firmly hypothesize that virtually all people are born with very strong tendencies to think crookedly about their important desires and preferences and to self-defeatingly escalate them into dogmatic, absolutistic shoulds, musts, oughts, demands, and commands. Their very nature is, first, to have probabilities and realistic expectations, and hopes of fulfilling their goals and wishes, and to feel appropriately sad, sorry, displeased, and frustrated when these are not met. But, being somewhat allergic to sticking to probability . . . when they have strong and paramount desires they very frequently, and often unconsciously or implic-

itly, escalate their longings into unconditional and rigid insistences and commands. By so doing, they create states of . . . "poor mental health." (Ellis, 1987, p. 373)

HUMAN EXPRESSION

The Rational-Emotive position places primary importance on *rational* thinking. Within this position, rational does not have any fixed definition. It is generally understood to refer to thoughts that aid and abet individuals in achieving their goals and purposes. By contrast, *irrational* is understood to refer to thoughts which prevent or block goal attainment (Dryden, 1984).

As thoughts are defined in terms of rational or irrational, emotions and behaviors are somewhat similarly defined. *Undisturbed* or *helpful* emotions and behaviors, like rational thoughts, refer to those that aid and abet individuals in achieving their goals and purposes. *Disturbed* or *hurtful* emotions and behaviors, like irrational thoughts, refer to those that prevent or block goal attainment.

The Rational-Emotive position posits that the three modes of human expression (cognitions, emotions, and behaviors) are inseparable and interactive, reciprocally influencing each other. Nonetheless, it is clear from Ellis' and other Rational-Emotive writers' assertions that the contribution of cognition is elucidated in the therapeutic milieu. For example, Ellis (1979, p. 45) affirmed the paramount role for thinking processes in facilitating therapeutic efforts from the Rational-Emotive postion: "major change in a person's philosophy can help bring about highly important and lasting changes in both emotions and behavior."

Undisturbed emotional functioning is presented as concurrent and/or prerequisite to undisturbed behavioral functioning. Walen, DiGiuseppe, and Wessler (1980) expound on this reasoning:

> As long as they remain upset (emotionally), their problem-solving skills will tend to be adversely affected and their ability to get what they want will be impaired. When disturbance (emotional) is reduced, interventions can focus on teaching clients how to choose or change their environments to minimize aversive conditions. (p. 22)

Authors' Note: It is important to recognize that the primary emphasis of cognition is an arbitrary one as is the secondary emphasis of emotion—for therapeutic purposes. Systemically, causation from a circular perspective would posit none of the three forms of human expression as inherently individually dominant; a "cause."

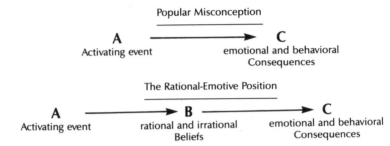

FIGURE 2.1   The ABC conceptualization of the Rational-Emotive position.

Adapted from: M. E. Bernard and M. R. Joyce, *Rational-emotive Therapy with Children and Adolescents: Theory, Treatment Strategies, Preventive Methods* (New York: Wiley, 1984): Copyright 1984 by Wiley. Reprinted by permission of the publisher.

The Rational-Emotive position is probably best known for its ABC conceptualization which describes the interplay between events (A), beliefs (B), and emotional and behavioral consequences (C). This conceptualization begins with an activating event (A). While the commonly accepted viewpoint is that A directly leads to C, the Rational-Emotive position is distinct in maintaining the important contributions of persons' beliefs (B) about what happened at A as leading to C. Moreover, beliefs are categorized with a focus on those that are *evaluative*. For example, consider the 8-year-old child who throws a temper tantrum when her parents decline to take her with them to a dinner party. As illustrated in Figure 2.1, the common misconception is that A, the activating event of not being allowed to accompany her parents (A) was directly followed by the child throwing the temper tantrum (C). According to the Rational-Emotive position, however, the child's evaluation (B) about the event follows A (e.g., "It's horribly unfair that I can't go. They must take me!"). By contrast, if just at the moment the child was being told she would not accompany her parents, and her belief was "I'd like to go, however, I'll have a good time with the babysitter," the response would not likely have been a temper tantrum.

The ABC conceptualization is useful in providing a simple and non-mysterious account of the interplay among events, beliefs, and consequences. It also offers an easily understood basis for stressing the contribution of beliefs. Because of its simplicity and because it corresponds to the majority of writings relative to the Rational-Emotive

Authors' Note: Figure 2.1 reflects the "linear" epistemology traditionally taken by many adhering to a Rational-Emotive position. Figure 2.2 below more accurately illustrates the ABC conceptualization from a systemic perspective: that is, "circular" as opposed to linear.

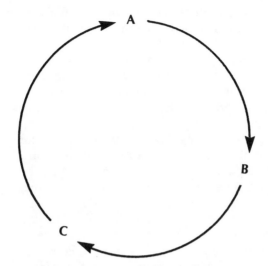

FIGURE 2.2   A family-systems perspective/circular epistemology of the ABCs
of the Rational-Emotive position.

position, the ABC conceptualization will be referred to throughout most
of this book. The model, however, is sometimes confusing, in part
because the distinction between A and B can be difficult to grasp; that
being when A is a cognition as opposed to an actual overt occurrence.
It is important to recall that the belief (B) referred to from the Rational-
Emotive perspective is a specific type of cognition—an *evaluation*.
Wessler and Wessler (1980) expanded the ABC conceptualization to an
8-step model to allow greater clarity in making these important distinctions.

Step 1 is a *stimulus configuration* which can be overt or covert. An overt
stimulus might be other persons' actions, an environmental event, or
the gain or loss of something tangible. Covert stimuli might include
bodily sensations (such as nausea) and thoughts (particularly memories
and anticipations).

Step 2 is *input and selection*. This refers to the portion of the stimulus
configuration that registers within one's sensory apparatus. It includes
the actions of the senses (visual images, noise, tastes, etc.) as well as
physiological processes that provide information about motive states
such as hunger and thirst. Also included herein are the assumed
physiological processes that serve the function of senses in providing

input from cognitive processes, leading to self-awareness. Thus, at a given instant, one might become aware of and attend to a smell, a sensation of hunger, and a thought.

Step 3 includes *definition and description*. It consists of distinctly cognitive perceptions, perception representing a process whereby incoming information is organized and categorized. Information about the experienced portion of the stimulus configuration is thus defined and then described through verbal statements. The statements may be overt or covert: "I see a dog; I hear music; I feel my stomach growling; I am thinking about going on vacation." Wessler and Wessler (1980) caution that Step 3 is not necessarily an essential step in their 8-step conceptualization because one may have a visual image of a dog, for instance, and immediately process that information at Step 5 (evaluation): "Dogs are dangerous (and therefore bad)." Or one might perceive a dog and immediately experience arousal at Step 6 (emotion), following a classical conditioning model. They suggest, however, that when Step 3 is omitted, one is most likely to process the information at Step 4.

Step 4, *interpretation*, refers to the making of inferences about the nonobservable aspects of the perceived portion of the stimulus configuration or about oneself. This involves going beyond the data at hand and includes such activities as guessing the intentions of others' actions, making forecasts about the data at hand, and assessing the implications of one's behaviors for self and others (Dryden, 1984). Wessler and Wessler (1980) offered the following examples to illustrate this step (S' = the perceived portion of the stimulus configuration): S' = a piece of wood; interpretation = the wood is hard (however, it might be soft balsa wood). S' = man walking toward post office with letter in hand; interpretation = he intends to mail the letter (however, he might be taking the letter home from the office). S' = a person does not speak to me; interpretation = I am not likable. (p. 6) Interpretations can be relatively general and enduring ("People cannot be trusted") or relatively specific and situational ("This person cannot be trusted"). Wessler and Wessler note that like Step 3, Step 4, interpretation, is not an essential step in their 8-step model. They further propose that humans tend to regularly make interpretations.

Step 5, *evaluation*, is the crucial step in this process from a Rational-Emotive position. Steps 1, 2, 3, and 4 comprise the A in the ABC conceptualization. Step 5 represents the B in the ABC conceptualization.

Authors' Note: Step 3 might be best understood as a purely descriptive, almost objective account of what occurred at Step 2.

Step 5 is composed of those cognitions that are *evaluative* in nature and indicate a sense of personal significance (the evaluation can be neutral, indecisive, or ambiguous; following, there would be no emotional response were this the case). These evaluative cognitions are categorized as being either *rational* or *irrational* beliefs. Step 5 and typical rational and irrational beliefs that comprise it will be expounded upon in the next section.

Step 6, *emotion*, refers to one's emotional experience. Wessler and Wessler (1980) identify this as "the arousal of the autonomic nervous system following nonneutral appraisal. The greater the deviation from neutral, the greater will be the arousal" (p. 7). In the ABC conceptualization, this step is called C, the emotional consequence.

Step 7 is the *action tendency*. This is the tendency to act in certain ways relative to a perceived stimulus: to approach that which is evaluated positively at step 5; to avoid or eliminate that which is evaluated negatively at step 5. This action tendency is referred to as the behavioral consequence portion of the C in the ABC conceptualization.

Step 8, *feedback*, represents the reinforcing consequences of steps 6 and 7. "Reinforcing consequences" simply means that rewards or penalties occur as a result of emotions and behaviors experienced and this information is fed back to reinstitute the entire process again in a deviation-reducing or deviation-amplifying manner (see Chapter 1: "Cybernetics and Circular Causality"). Humans, operating on hedonistic principles, tend to repeat actions that bring satisfaction and eliminate those that do not. Step 8 does not have a corresponding letter in the ABC conceptualization, but because it is a significant factor from a systemic perspective, it is an important addition to that conceptualization.

RATIONAL AND IRRATIONAL BELIEFS

The Rational-Emotive position addresses itself primarily to two forms of evaluative cognitions at step 5 in the model just described. These are called *rational* and *irrational* beliefs. In terms of the model, rational beliefs are matters of personal significance that are relative in nature and adaptively appraise a perceived stimulus configuration. When humans evaluate in a relative manner and adaptively appraise, they experience emotions which indicate pleasure; sometimes, they also experience emotions which indicate displeasure such as sadness, annoyance, and concern. While these latter emotions are not necessarily desirable, they are considered appropriate responses relative to negative activating events at A in that they do not significantly interfere with the pursuit of personal goals or, if these goals are forever blocked, the selection and pursuit of new goals. These "helpful" emotions (relative to the activating event) accompany rational beliefs which are nonabsolute, adaptively appraising statements of personal significance (Dryden, 1984).

Irrational beliefs are matters of personal significance that are stated in absolute nonadaptive terms relative to the activitating event at A. Emotions accompanying irrational beliefs include expressions of depression, anger, and guilt. These expressions of "hurtful" emotion are seen as going hand in hand with exaggerated evaluations and thus are maladaptive relative to even a negative activating event in that they generally impede the pursuit of personal goals. For example, even if persons might acquire what they deem they absolutely "must" have, they generally do not experience lasting satisfaction because of the accompanying prospect of potentially losing it (Dryden, 1984). Ellis (1982) identified rational beliefs as contributing to "helpful" problem-solving behaviors while irrational beliefs are seen as contributing to "hurtful" problem-maintaining or intensifying behaviors.

The major irrational beliefs people have been observed to hold, contributing to disturbed, hurtful emotional and behavioral consequences tend to derive from a basic *demandingness* or *must* (Ellis, 1980, pp. 5–7):

1. I *must* do well and win approval for my performance, or else I rate as a rotten person.
2. Others *must* treat me considerately and kindly in precisely the way I want them to treat me; if they don't society and the universe should severely blame, damn, and punish them for their inconsiderateness.
3. Conditions under which I live *must* get arranged so that I get practically everything I want comfortably, quickly, and easily, and get virtually nothing I don't want.

With regard to demandingness evaluations, Ellis (1971) also stated:

Practically all 'emotional disturbance' stems from *demanding* or *whining* instead of from *wanting* or *desiring*. People who feel anxious, depressed or hostile don't merely *wish* or *prefer* something, but also *command, dictate, insist* that they achieve this thing. Typically, . . . they *dictate* that life and world be easy, enjoyable, and unfrustrating; and they *manufacture* overrebelliousness, self-pity, and inertia when conditions are difficult. (p. 168)

Thus, whenever people begin to feel and act extremely disturbed and upset, the disturbance usually begins with a wish or desire that gets blocked or thwarted in some way. The wish itself is quite adaptive relative to the pursuit of personal goals, but disturbance and dysfunction come about when the desire becomes escalated into an absolute *demand* (e.g., "I must get that job I applied for!"). Demands can normally be recognized by cue words such as "must," "have to," "should," "ought," and "need."

The Rational-Emotive position further stresses that three primary forms of equally irrational thinking emanate from this basic demandingness ("must") (Ellis, 1980):

1. *Devastation Beliefs/Awfulizing* ("It is awful, or terrible that I am not doing as I must.")
2. *Discomfort Disturbance Beliefs/I can't stand-it-itis* ("I can't stand, can't bear the things that are happening to me that must not happen.")
3. *Denigration Beliefs/Worthlessness* ("I am a worthless person if I don't do as well and win as much approval as I must.")

Devastation or *awfulizing* evaluations exaggerate the negative consequences of a situation. Ellis (1971) described these in stating:

> Just about every time you feel disturbed or upset—instead of merely displeased, frustrated, or disappointed—you are stoutly convincing yourself that something is *awful*, rather than inconvenient or disadvantageous. . . .
> When you *awfulize* or *catastrophize* about reality, you are setting up an unverifiable, magical, unempirical hypothesis. (p. 168)

Therefore, when people experience extremely upsetting emotions that tend to impede any progress they might make in pursuit of personal goals, they are evaluating bad circumstances as much more than just bad; but rather as the "end of the world" (e.g., "I cannot go on living if I don't get this job," with the implication that life would be utterly "devastating"). These exaggerated devastation evaluations can typically be identified by individuals' use of such descriptors as "horrible," "terrible," "awful," and "unbearable."

Discomfort disturbance or *I can't stand-it-itis* evaluations typically arise when people begin by desiring or preferring that things go easy for them. Discomfort disturbance evaluations occur when the desire is escalated to a demand: "Things must be easy for me!" This demand to be comfortable tends to prevent people from doing the persistent and, at times, hard work that it takes to attain many personal goals and life satisfactions. The ability to tolerate discomfort and frustration, not for their own sake, but so that constructive movement toward goal attainment and greater life satisfaction can be realized is considered a primary criterion of psychological health within the Rational-Emotive position (Dryden, 1984). It is central to the acquisition of a philosophy of long-range hedonism: that being the pursuit of meaningful longer-term goals while tolerating the deprivation of attractive shorter-term goals which are self-defeating in the longer term.

Denigration evaluations are maladaptive appraisals of self and others. Damnation involves a process of rating the totality of oneself or another. Statements such as "I am a failure," "He is no good," or the reverse, "I am a success," "He is a super person" represent examples of denigration evaluations. These statements all include an evaluative label applied to the total person. The effect of these evaluations is to potentially contribute to, on the one hand, the debilitating emotions of guilt, shame, or anxiety, or on the other hand, falsely self/other-enhancing emotions of pride and euphoria. Unfortunately, these falsely self-enhancing emotions accompany the same belief as the debilitating emotions—that persons can be totally worthwhile or worthless. This point was summarized aptly by Wessler and Wessler (1980) with the biblical quotation: "Pride goeth before a fall" (p. 45).

Whenever people engage in self/other rating, they typically focus on a specific characteristic or behavior, evaluate it according to a standard of desirability or worth, and then apply this evaluation to oneself or another. For example, one may believe that it is undesirable or bad to make mistakes. Such is an adaptive evaluation in that usually there are negative consequences which accompany making a mistake. However, carrying the evaluation of the mistaken action to an evaluation of one's total being can be quite maladaptive in terms of pursuing personal goals. "I did a bad thing; therefore I am a bad person" offers little potential for correction and revised pursuit of one's goals. The Rational-Emotive position advocates that persons evaluate their actions and the accompanying effects of their actions; benefits and goal attainment clearly accompany some actions more so than others. This position, however, also advocates that persons minimize their tendency to leap to total evaluations of self and others based on these same actions. A byword of the Rational-Emotive position is "Rate the act, not the actor" (Wessler & Wessler, 1980).

Ellis (1973) has asserted that the rational alternative to denigration is acceptance or acknowledgement. Acknowledgement suggests that notions of human worth are simply not adaptive in pursuit of personal goals. Humans are fallible creatures who can never attain perfection; acknowledgement of this will tend to allow them to enjoy present achievements (without undue concern for their eventual dissipation) and not be downtrodden by their mistakes (for the future always offers new opportunities).

BELIEFS AND RELATIONSHIP INTERACTIONS

The Rational-Emotive position advocates relationship interactions that provide long-range hedonistic satisfaction—that is, pleasurable experience—for the individuals involved (DiGiuseppe & Zeeve, 1985). In general, it encourages people to experience pleasure and avoid or eliminate pain to the degree that is possible without inhibiting adaptive goal attainment; to interact in ways they believe will help achieve these goals mindful that this is done within the context of a social world (Dryden, 1984). In line with this view, the Rational-Emotive position proposes that persons actively participate in relationship interactions that promise or provide the most hedonistic satisfaction, particularly those interactions that continue to furnish it over time (Ellis, 1982; Ellis & Becker, 1982; Ellis & Harper, 1975).

The Rational-Emotive position distinguishes between absolute and relative satisfaction in relationship interactions (DiGiuseppe & Zeeve, 1985). *Relative satisfaction* refers to the degree of satisfaction or dissatisfaction experienced in relationship interactions when evaluating those interactions against possible alternatives. *Absolute satisfaction*, by contrast, refers to the degree of satisfaction or dissatisfaction experienced in relationship interactions when evaluating those interactions against some ideal, absolute standard whose attainment is highly unlikely, if not impossible. Absolute satisfaction can rarely, if ever, be experienced and thus such a goal almost invariably accompanies unsatisfactory relationship interactions. DiGiuseppe and Zeeve (1985) term this latter state *relationship disturbance.*

Relationship disturbance reflects the irrational beliefs on the part of relationship members. Evaluations of the relationship revolve around beliefs that unless the relationship is utterly ideal (there is a demand that it *must* be), it is utterly bad (which, of course, is devastating). Because it is not, they themselves or other members tend to be seen as all bad (and thus are damned forever for their failure). Further, the discomfort experienced is "unbearable" ("We can't stand it!). The emotional upset which accompanies such evaluations is likely to interfere with any relative satisfactions that the relationship might actually be able to offer.

Relative satisfaction with relationship interactions is a desirable goal and reflects rational beliefs on the part of relationship members. Relative dissatisfaction also reflects rational beliefs on the part of relationship members. Relative dissatisfaction with relationship interactions may occur for any number of reasons, none of which have anything to do with psychopathology, deep-seated conflicts, or irrational beliefs. For example, a marital relationship considered very satisfying when a couple was without children may very rationally be evaluated as less so when the responsibilities of parenthood impinge upon time formally available for marital pleasures.

Whatever the beginnings of relative relationship dissatisfaction, it is accompanied by negative emotions that, though they might be quite intense, are nonetheless adaptive and thus appropriate to the activating event. Parents who are rationally evaluating their children's problem behaviors as undesirable, disappointing, and acknowledge their fallibility, will experience sadness, annoyance, and concern about mutual interactions with their children. They will not feel inappropriately and dysfunctionally depressed, angry, guilty, or panicked. These parents' behavior will likely fall into the adaptive range: they will try to improve relationship interactions by various means; or if improvement is not feasible, attempt to make the best of an apparently bad situation.

Relative relationship dissatisfaction need not lead to relationship disturbance. Relationship members may be quite dissatisfied with their relationship interactions and this dissatisfaction will not be escalated unless irrational evaluations evolve. Where both dissatisfaction and disturbance are present, however, the Rational-Emotive position holds that relationship disturbance is best addressed prior to dealing with issues of relationship dissatisfaction. There are several reasons for this: first, relative relationship dissatisfaction will almost always be intensified by an overlay of disturbance. Members' emotional accompanyment to any given activating event will be more intense and negative than it would be if they were able to remain relatively rational in their evaluations. Their subjective experience of the event will be more unpleasant and stressful than it would be otherwise. Further, members will be faced with both the activating event accompanying the dissatisfaction (which itself may be rationally quite unpleasant) and the additional aversive matter of dealing with the disturbing, maladaptive emotions accompanying irrational evaluations of that event. Disturbance can be seen as "turning up the volume" on whatever difficulties relationship members might experience (DiGiuseppe & Zeeve, 1985). Second, it tends to be extremely difficult to identify and operationalize specific dissatisfaction evaluations until the overlay of disturbance evaluations have been dealt with. Third, potential solutions helpful in addressing dissatisfaction issues are unlikely to be maximally effective when relationship members are emotionally upset. With regard to this latter point, DiGiuseppe and Zeeve (1985) offered the following caution relative to behavioral contracting with couples in marital therapy:

> It is difficult, for example, to get angry couples to comply with behavioral contracting procedures; angry people see little reason to try to please those with whom they are angry, and see similarly little reason to stop engaging in behaviors designed to punish their offending mates. Further, angry people often construe—or misconstrue—their mate's compliance with a contract as mere manipulative attempts to win over the therapist and get him or her to take sides. (p. 65)

RATIONALITY AS A RELATIONSHIP PHILOSOPHY

The Rational-Emotive position toward rationality as a relationship philosophy posits two explicit values: *survival* and *enjoyment*. The evaluations persons make can be appraised against these values in the search for rational thinking. Evaluations that promote these values can be defined as rational; those evaluations that do not can be defined as irrational. Goals for a relationship philosophy of rationality, therefore, might include living life with as much enjoyment as possible given the limitations of the human body and the physical and social world; living peacefully within that world; and relating intimately with certain people in that world (Walen, DiGiuseppe, & Wessler, 1980). Accompanying these values are several assertions relating to uniqueness, hedonism, responsibility in decisionmaking, and lifestyle (Wessler & Wessler, 1980).

Rationality as a relationship philosophy values the uniqueness of all humans. Forcing a particular mold on anyone is strongly discouraged. Humans are fallible, and even with the "best" intentions, they are prone to make mistakes. Rationality as a relationship philosophy asserts the right to err, the right to be wrong by any standard, for that is a fact of human nature. However, the mistake maker is best not valued or devalued for being what he or she is, a unique human being.

A second important assertion relating to rationality as a relationship philosophy is *hedonism*. Hedonism can be thought of as merely seeking pleasure and avoiding pain, but such an assertion would not necessarily lead to *continued* life enjoyment and survival. Deriving pleasure from some action with harmful side effects will eventually eliminate the pleasure. Thus, alcohol or drugs used to excess provide considerable pleasure in the short-term but much more pain than pleasure in the long term. Because some short-term pleasures may work against the other main value, survival, the Rational-Emotive position advocates moderation.

The term used by Rational-Emotive writers for this moderation is *hedonic calculus*, a concept taken from the pragmatic philosophers of the nineteenth century (Walen, DiGiuseppe, & Wessler, 1980). Hedonic calculus refers to the evaluation of whether the pleasure of today is likely to backfire some way in the future. Conversely, if persons lived only for the future, they might pass up a great deal of current enjoyment; the Rational-Emotive position advocates noncompulsively seeking a compromise solution that sacrifices neither the present nor the future (Walen et al., 1980).

Being unique fallible hedonists who are mindful of the future, rationality as a relationship philosophy recognizes that persons are faced with continual choices. Decisions are constantly there to be made—some major, some minor, most in between. Rationality as a relationship philosophy asserts taking personal responsibility for decisions made with the understanding that choice is limited within the social, physical, and economic constraints of one's world. Ellis (1978) offered comment on this relative to the Rational-Emotive position as being indeterministic:

> Deterministic theories see individuals as not responsible for their behavior, as the pawns of society, heredity, or both. Indeterministic theories put emphasis on self-direction and place control within the person. (the Rational Emotive position) . . . stands mainly in the indeterministic camp. But it sees choice as *limited*. It hypothesizes that the more rationally people think and behave, the less deterministic they act. But rationality has its limits and hardly leads to completely free, healthy, or utopian existences. (p. 307)

Dealings with others can be based on anticipating the consequences of one's actions. What is rational is specific to each situation; there are no absolute rights or wrongs. Experience shows, however, that if others are treated unfairly, they will eventually retaliate in kind. Likewise, if they are treated fairly, they will similarly reciprocate. Hence, it would be unwise to exploit and act harmfully toward others. It would not be wrong in an absolute sense, but rather in the sense that it would likely prevent the attainment of maximum life enjoyment and threaten survival. Thus, decisions about relating to others are not based solely on moral commandments of right or wrong but in terms of how one's actions affect personal goals which include beneficial relationships with others. Moral commandments can provide helpful guidelines to consider, however, actions are best based on situational requirements and conditions.

Finally, rationality as a relationship philosophy advocates certain styles of living—styles implicit in the notions "It is better to have loved and lost than never to have loved at all" and "What's worth having is worth striving for" (Wessler & Wessler, 1980). "Loved and lost" relates to the benefits of risk taking, not risks that endanger survival but those that might lead to situational rejection or failure. Risk taking accompanies a hedonistic philosophy. To maximize pleasure means getting, as much as possible, what one wants. (Some of what one wants may be gotten without trying, however, the probability of doing so is much less when left to chance.) To seek to get what one wants means to risk failing. Without risking failing, success will rarely be experienced.

Related to risk-taking is the effort involved in taking risks. "What is worth having is worth striving for" asserts basic values and goals can be best achieved by *actively* pursuing them. Although in some instances, the process of striving can be pleasurable, in most it involves discomfort and at times drudgery. Long-term goal attainment almost always requires effort. Wessler and Wessler (1980, p. 61) describe the reverse of this position as being "I shouldn't have to do anything that is unpleasant or uncomfortable, and I'd sooner maintain the status quo than risk discomfort." While anyone clearly has a right to live by this latter belief, it would likely lead to significant dissatisfaction by blocking pursuit of longer term enjoyment and possibly survival.

In summary, Rational-Emotive position advocates a nondogmatic, nonabsolutistic relationship philosophy that is socially responsible. This philosophy will be nurtured by answers to the question, "Will my actions help both me and others or harm me or others?" Rationally responsible acts are seen as those which are both prosocial and proself. In essense, the "Golden Rule": Do unto others as you would have them do unto you.

3

Context, Cognitions, and Change

Theories offer the field of family therapy explanations as to how behavior develops and how it might be changed when problematic. They are not abstractions divorced from clinical practice, nor collections of heuristic but unrelated hypotheses. For family therapy, theory serves as a basis for the conceptual understanding of family systems and how they operate. Further, the use of theory as an organizing framework provides therapists with strategies for treatment. And while some therapists eschew the use of theory altogether, claiming that good therapy is intuitive, the effective therapist needing only to be "a real self" (Whitaker, 1976), most find a well-defined theoretical perspective invaluable as a guide for deliberate and decisive therapeutic action (Nichols, 1984).

Chapter 1 addressed the family systems perspective as conceptualized by General Systems Theory and more particularly, cybernetics. The shift in the behavioral sciences from exclusive concerns with individual character to a focus on interactional context was marked by the development of the concepts emanating from this theoretical perspective. Formerly baffling observations became better understood through this theory which emphasized circular, rather than linear causality. What might be seen as "reality" for humans, within the behavioral sciences at least, thus became contextual. Human beings do not simply live in a world of facts, still less in a billiard-ball world of forces and impacts, but in a world of facts and meanings in which "what a thing is" involves and includes what it *means*—its significance. What anything "is" depends upon the context in which "it" is found; that context being part of what "it" is. The same "thing" in different contexts will mean something different and therefore will *be* different (O'Hanlon & Wilk, 1987). Two fingers raised in a "V" during World War II meant "victory" à la win the war. The same gesture during the Vietnam era meant "peace" à la end the hostility, not win it.

Chapter 2 reviewed the Rational-Emotive position. This theory advocates an emphasis on cognition in the therapeutic milieu. Although the three modes of human expression (cognition, emotion, and behavior) are seen as inseparable and interactive in reciprocally influencing each other, cognition is differentiated for purposes of the treatment of human dysfunction.

The Rational-Emotive position accepts (either explicitly or implicitly) the majority of those concepts emanating from the family-systems perspective. The significant difference between the Rational-Emotive position and the family-systems perspective is their traditional focus relative to the unit of treatment. The family-systems perspective has almost exclusively focused conceptually on the context—the family system—with individual family members' functioning (e.g., their cognitions) taking a less primary place. Interventions emanating from this perspective are designed to disrupt current dysfunctional family interactions. In contrast, the Rational-Emotive position has traditionally focused on individuals and their cognitions first with secondary focus on the context, the family system. Unfortunately, this has tended to result in little being written relative to the Rational-Emotive position as practiced with families. It is the authors' present belief and experience that this has led to and reflects a paucity of Rational-Emotive "family therapy." We critique a quote by Ellis to illustrate this. First, as stated by Ellis (1982):

> While agreeing with these basic views of systems theory—oriented family therapy, RET would offer a few caveats as follows: (1) Focusing on wholeness, organization, and relationship among family members is important, but can be over-done. Families become disturbed not merely because of *their* organization but because of the serious personal problems of the family members. Unless, therefore, these are considered and dealt with, *too*, any changes that are likely to occur through changing the family system are likely to be superficial and unlasting and family therapy will tend to be wasteful. (2) Family-systems therapy tends to require an active–directive therapist who makes clearcut interventions and who engages in a great deal of problem solving. RET is highly similar in these respects. But most family-system therapists tend to ignore the phenomenological and self-disturbing aspects of family members' problems. . . (3) Because they focus largely on family situations and interpersonal communications and problems, family therapists, for all of their cleverness and use of many cognitive methods, usually miss the main reasons behind

most people's emotional and behavioral problems: namely, their absolutistic *musts* and *shoulds* and their other irrational beliefs. In this respect,
systems family therapy is partially effective but still superficial. (pp. 312–313)

The following is our contrasting critique through a paraphrase of Ellis'
quote: While agreeing with the basic views of the Rational-Emotive position, a few caveats might be offered as follows: (1) Focusing on the beliefs
of individual family members can be over-done. Families become
disturbed not merely because of the serious personal problems of the
individual members, but also because of the family's organization and
disorganization. Unless, therefore, these latter are considered and dealt
with, *too*, any changes that are likely to occur through changes in individual members' beliefs are likely to be superficial and not lasting. (2)
The Rational-Emotive position tends to require an active–directive
therapist who makes clearcut interventions and who engages in a great
deal of problem solving. The family-systems perspective is highly similar
in these respects. But most Rational-Emotive therapists tend to give too
little attention to contextual contributions to family members' problems.
(3) Because they focus largely on individuals' absolutistic musts and
shoulds and other irrational beliefs, Rational-Emotive therapists usually
miss the equally contributing bases for most persons' emotional and
behavioral problems: namely, the context within which they find
themselves.

The shift from individual psychotherapy to family therapy requires
new ways of thinking. The family-systems perspective provides useful
theoretical models in General Systems theory and cybernetics. While
we might assert our posture as "correct," recursive complementarity
presupposes that Ellis is "correct" as well. When early systemic thinkers
initially began to claim the family as an organic whole, they were met
with a good deal of resistance from the prevailing therapeutic community. In the face of this resistance, they fought hard, defending their
new perspective with religious zeal. This insistence on focusing only
on contextual dynamics permitted a consolidation of ideas about
systemic functioning and the development of innovative, powerful
techniques. But all new perspectives carry with them the liability of
selective absorption and dichotomous, either/or thinking. Thus, while
sharpening their appreciation of social relationships, systemic pro-
ponents tended to ignore the individual (Nichols, 1987).

Many systemic theorists and therapists seem to have forgotten that
seeing a family as a "system" is only one of many possible ways of
thinking; instead, they tend to take it as a fundamental reality. Nichols

(1987) communicated his personal experience in accepting this "fallacy of misplaced concreteness": mistaking concrete reality for abstractions which may be useful in studying reality:

> As I learned more about family therapy . . . I put aside my earlier analytic training and concentrated on the interactions between people rather than on the individual characteristics of the people interacting. But over the years I've become aware that ignoring the subjective experience and private motivations of individual family members could be as limiting as ignoring the effect of family-interaction patterns. I discovered that one person's symptoms may reflect *both* that person's disturbance and the relationship's disturbance. (p. 36)

The unity of the family system can best be seen by stepping back, blurring our focus of the individual members in order to see the whole. Unfortunately, in this process of stepping back far enough to see the whole system, sometimes sight of the individual is lost. The reverse is similarly unfortunate in that moving in too close to the individual loses sight of the context within which he or she exists. This chapter seeks to acknowledge the simultaneous communication being offered by the family-systems perspective and the Rational-Emotive position. It presents the concept of "the meaningful new" represented here by the Mental Research Institute (MRI) strategy, a theory of change, that equally and conceptually complements both RET and family-systems perspectives. The cybernetic system evolving therein we identify as Rational-Emotive Family Therapy (REFT): a new "clinical epistemology." As an essentially clinical rather than academic discipline, clinical epistemology is intended not as an evolving body of theory or research, but as an evolving set of practical, clinical procedures. O'Hanlon and Wilk (1987) offered further explanation in noting:

> Clinical epistemology is the conceptual analysis of the effect on psycho-therapeutic practice and outcome of shifts in a therapist's presuppositions about the nature of human beings, the human mind, human difficulties, and the resolution of those difficulties. The clinical application of this conceptual analysis involves bringing about therapeutic resolutions of difficulties by altering a client's presuppositions, either directly or indirectly, thereby creating a context for effective psychotherapy. Thus, in applying clinical epistemology to therapeutic practice, we examine and challenge both therapists' (i.e., our own) and our clients' implicit beliefs and unexamined assumptions and conclusions about their "problems," about what (if anything) caused them, and about what will resolve them. (p. 12)

The Mental Research Institute (MRI) strategy, a theory of change prescribed by Watzlawick, Weakland, and Fisch in their book *Change: Principles of Problem Formation and Problem Resolution* (1974) and by Fisch, Weakland, and Segal in their book *The Tactics of Change* (1982) is perhaps one of the most efficient problem-solving approaches in the history of psychotherapy. The MRI strategy is founded in cybernetic theory. It focuses primarily on the processes of communication operating within human systems. And while each has its own unique jargon, the Rational-Emotive position and the MRI strategy are remarkably compatible on epistemological as well as practical levels.

EPISTEMOLOGY

Every psychotherapeutic theory, either explicitly or implicitly, suggests how it should be viewed in the context of other viewpoints. Stances range on a continuum from "the ultimate truth as revealed by God" to "this might help get us through the day." The MRI strategy takes great care to emphasize its incompleteness. It is normally presented as being only one of many ways to view human beings, and "within this view, theories, and assumptions do not represent 'truth' " (Fisch, Weakland, Watzlawick, Segal, Hoebel, & Deardorff, 1975, p. 3). Likewise, Ellis (1987) asserted relative to the Rational-Emotive position:

> . . . much room for development exists. . . . If this were not so, . . . Rational-Emotive Therapy would be dogmatic rather than scientific. Science only has tentative hypotheses, which are always subject to change and revision. Let us hope that, in this sense . . . RET will remain scientific— ever open to new developments and advances. (p. 278)

Although potentially incomplete, the role of theory in the practice of psychotherapy is considered to be of paramount importance within the MRI strategy. As Fisch et al. state:

> Any theory of psychotherapy is essentially a set of assumptions and therapy without theory means only that the assumptions are not stated. Whether explicit or, even more importantly, implicit, assumptions dictate what we do and do not do with our patients. (1975, p. 2)

The Rational-Emotive position's view of the role of theory in psychotherapy is remarkably similar. For example, Ellis (1973) proposed:

It is not *what* system the therapist uses that helps the client, but the fact that he *has* a pretty well integrated approach to personality formation, even if his approach is largely wrong. For the client's system of thinking and behaving, and especially evaluating himself as a human being, is so palpably disorganzied and unintegrated, or else is so rigidly aligned so that it can only produce self-defeating results, that virtually *any* other systematic approach to personality will bring better results if he starts to follow it. (p. 188)

Historically, both the Rational-Emotive position and the MRI strategy have been perceived as revolutionary avant garde and have introduced radically different ways of conceptualizing the practice of psychotherapy. The MRI strategy introduced to psychotherapy a new epistemology with its application of cybernetic thinking to the therapeutic process. Likewise, the Rational-Emotive position represented at the time of its original introduction a significant shift in the way psychotherapy was practiced. Writers from both have filled pages that took the then pre-vailing psychoanalytic thinking to task and asserted that "conventional/ traditional" psychoanalytic therapeutic approaches were actually part of many clients' problems. Thus, both the Rational-Emotive position and the MRI strategy have been rebels within the context of psycho-therapeutic theories. They also represent a significant shift with their emphasis on interaction as opposed to isolation.

Mainstream psychology historically sets out to prove that, like physics, it was a true science. Initially, that model of what a science should be primarily came from Newtonian physics, which posited a linear, cause–effect epistemology. Freud asserted that he had discovered the "true science" of the mind which allowed a therapist to pursue that linear, cause–effect chain in following a neurosis back to its origins in early childhood. Any psychotherapeutic theory that has subsequently at-tempted to set a different epistemological course has been obliged to address this originating psychoanalytic epistemology. In the literature of the MRI strategy and the Rational-Emotive position there are extended explicit and implicit references assaulting linear thinking.

For example, Watzlawick and Weakland (1977), illustrated how the linear epistemology of psychoanalysis and the cybernetic circular epistemology of the MRI strategy would lead to two very different ther-apeutic stances. Working from a linear model, the therapist logically (according to the practices which emanate from this epistemology) would delve into the client's past to discover the "cause" of the presenting problem. The epistemological interrogative would be "why?" With the assistance of the therapist, the client would be led to see the cause–effect chain and thus would acquire "insight." Watzlawick and Weakland (1977, p. xiv) summarized this process: In accordance with *this* theory of the nature of psychiatric disorders he will, quite correctly and consistently, treat the woman's case in monadic, intrapsychic isolation and on the basis of the above-mentioned epistemology of a linear, unidirectional causality.

They then contrasted this with cybernetic epistemology:

> If, on the other hand, he takes into account the marital interaction as described . . . he will attempt to discover *what* is going on here and now and not *why* the spouses' respective attitudes evolved in their individual pasts. He will identify their pattern of interaction as well as their attempted solutions (the more-of-the-same quality of their escalating behaviors) and he will then design the most appropriate and effective therapeutic intervention into the present functioning of this human system. (p. xiv)

A comparison of these comments with epistemological assertions found in the Rational-Emotive literature offers significant similarity in the two points of view. For example, Ellis (1982) wrote:

> Regardless of how family members originally became (or made themselves) disturbed, they feel upset today because they are *still* indoctrinating themselves with the same kinds of iBs [*irrational Beliefs*] that they originated in the past. Even if they learned some of these iBs from their parents and other early socializing agents, they *keep* repeating and retaining them today. (p. 310)

Both the Rational-Emotive position and the MRI strategy place little value in the "old" linear epistemology. Both also place little value in the utility of the historical "why" in claiming that therapists will find more meaningful solutions to the therapeutic puzzle in the "here and now." Both epistemologies lead the therapist to think in terms of patterns to best explain current functioning. With the epistemological compatibility of the two now offered, the balance of this chapter will address how the MRI strategy, as a theory of change, promotes the simultaneous perception of cognition and context and thus, a new clinical epistemology in the manner of Rational Emotive Family Therapy.

THE THEORY OF LOGICAL TYPES AND
THE DOUBLE BIND

The initial MRI work was a project funded by a grant from the National Institute of Health for the study of schizophrenia "designed to investigate the nature of human communications, specifically the nature and function of paradoxical communication, as it could be understood deductively through application of the Theory of Logical Types (Wilder, 1979, p. 172). The theory was extrapolated from Whitehead and Russell's *Principia Mathematica* (1910). The theory of logical types focuses on differentiating between classes and members of classes. The following discussion illustrates how this theory might be applied to the study of behavior:

> Bateson's group observed that the behavior of the monkeys in the San Francisco Zoo was similar when they fought and when they played (e.g., rushing at each other with teeth bared). Somehow, in a split second, the monkeys would seem to discern the intentions of another simian who rushed at them with teeth exposed. According to the theory of types, the differentiation would be made in terms of whether the manifested behavior was a *member of the class* of behaviors called *playing* or if it was a *member of the class* of behaviors called *fighting*. Obviously monkeys that were unable to make such differentiations would create, through their inappropriate responses, many problems both for themselves and for the other monkeys. (McKelvie, 1987, p. 153)

Similarly, in humans, the MRI project speculated that schizophrenics had failed to develop the ability to accurately differentiate the meaning (class) of communications sent by others and subsequently developed their own idiosyncratic formula for communicating with others. To further understand this phenomenon, the interactions of schizophrenics and their families were observed. The following represents a prototype of these interactions:

> Father comes to visit hospitalized schizophrenic daughter, runs to hug father; father reflexively moves away from daughter; daughter confused steps back; father, with great concern, says "Now don't be afraid of showing your emotions."

Confusion occurs because the daughter erroneously assumes that her father's actions belong to the class of "let's be intimate," as his entreaty that she share suggests, when in effect, the "meta-message" or class of his behavior is "keep your distance." The recipients of such conflicting messages are placed in a "bind" if they do not recognize the mixed messages they are receiving. Unable to respond to the conflicting messages in the illustration above, the daughter could leave the field and develop her own private scheme for communicating with others. While from the daughter's standpoint this could be considered an adaptation to a perceived impossible situation, to others her idiosyncratic approach to communication would be disruptive and likely labeled as pathological. Based on numerous observations of interactions such as this, the double-bind theory of schizophrenia was developed (Bateson, Jackson, Haley, & Weakland, 1956).

The MRI strategy, recognizing the impact of these paradoxical communication patterns as exemplified in the double-bind paradigm, identifies a class of "be spontaneous" paradoxes which, given the above conditions, frequently lead to pathological communication states. For example, "If you really loved me, I wouldn't have to tell you to call when you're going to be late." Such "be spontaneous" requests are impossible to satisfy. If the receiver of the message does not follow the injunction, his or her behavior is taken as a blatant example of purposeful rebellion. If followed, the action will be met with: "You only did it because I told you." Thus there is no way to respond successfully to the request of the sender (Watzlawick, Weakland, & Fisch, 1974).

THE CALCULUS OF COMMUNICATION

Originally published in *Pragmatics of Human Communication* (Watzlawick, Beavin, & Jackson, 1967), the MRI strategy's assumptions about human communication which occurs within social systems were generated with the desire to develop axioms that might form the basis for a "calculus of communication" about the interpersonal implications of communication. The following assumptions make up this calculus:

1. Communication always takes place within a context which must be taken into account in order to understand the meaning of messages. For example, said in the context of a classroom setting, the simple sentence "Where did you get that idea?" has a significantly different meaning than if uttered in a criminal court.

2. In the presence of another, all behavior is communicative. We cannot not communicate. For example, when in another's presence, an im-

mense amount of information is exchanged even before a word is spoken just by the fact of being together (e.g., nonverbal messages such as "she appears upset").

3. Communication is an interpersonal process. Who is the sender and who is the receiver is a moot point. Both participate equally in the reciprocal process of communication. During the process of communicating there is an ongoing series of interactions with each participant acting on and reacting to the flow of information coming from the other (e.g., "When I said that, she laughed" or "I wonder what he's trying to tell me now").

4. Meaning depends on how the communicational sequence is emphasized (e.g., "Is the rat being trained to press a lever after being presented a stimulus, or is the experimenter being trained to deliver food after the rat presses the lever?"). How the flow of information is emphasized will determine the meaning attributed to it (e.g., "She's smiling so she must be enjoying what I am saying" versus "This is amusing! But he's making somewhat of a fool out of himself").

5. Communication may be either symmetrical or complementary. Both symmetrical and complementary communications can be stable and functional or both can be unstable and pathological. Symmetrical communications occur between equals where participants all assume that they have an equal right to initiate action, criticize, and the like. Complementary interactions occur when the relationship is not equal; typically there is a one-up and a one-down position. It is important to recognize one-up and one-down as descriptive terms, not evaluative.

6. Communication is always multilevel. One level is the report level which is concerned with factual information; the other is the command level which indicates how the information is to be taken. "What are you doing?" is a simple request for information on the report level; however, were it being spoken by an angry employer to an erring employee or by an admiring student to a professor the sentence might carry different messages on the command level about how the message is to be taken (i.e., criticism vs. admiration).

The relationship between speakers is a factor that significantly affects how communications are responded to, particularly the command aspects. For example, a therapist whose aim is to help clients express their feelings would likely respond to a husband who is crying by listening empathically and encouraging him to continue to express his thoughts and feelings. The man's wife, on the other hand, might well be threatened and upset by his display of "weakness" and try to "cheer him up" by telling him that the problem doesn't really exist, or by suggesting ways for him to solve it. In this situation, the therapist can listen to the man's feelings without hearing (or responding to) a command to "do something about them." The wife feels threatened and obligated by the inferred command, and so cannot simply listen.

This command aspect functions to define relationships. "Daddy, Lou is picking on me" suggests that the speaker accepts a one-down (complementary) relationship with Lou, but insists that father intercede to settle any problems. This defining is often obscured because it is not necessarily consciously deliberate, and, depends on how it is received. In better-functioning relationships, this defining aspect recedes into the background. Conversely, problematic relationships are characterized by frequent struggles about the nature of the relationship (Nichols, 1984).

FAMILY RULES

In families, command messages are patterned as *rules* (Jackson, 1965). A major assertion of the MRI strategy is that *"the family is a rule-governed system;* that its members behave among themselves in an organized, repetitive manner and that this patterning of behaviors can be abstracted as governing principles of family life" (Jackson, 1977, p. 6). The family is seen as a social unit characterized by ongoing relationships which are stabilized by commonly adhered-to rules. The family members are not necessarily aware of these rules, the norms that govern their system. These rules evolve over time as activators for homeostatic mechanisms to ensure that behavior does not deviate too far from the family norms.

Most family rules are unwritten and covertly stated. That is, they are inferences that all family members make relative to the repetitive patterns they observe occurring around them. "Go to mother when you have a problem; she's more understanding." "It's best to ask father for money first thing in the morning when he's in a hurry to leave for work." "Stay away from their bedroom on weekend mornings; they sleep late." A common family rule, unstated but understood by all, is that decisions are made by parents and handed down to children. In some families, however, all family members learn that they can state their opinions freely. Parents also learn and adhere to covert rules: son is active in athletics, but it isn't something daughter would enjoy; child A can be depended on to do well in school, but child B cannot; child C is not trustworthy with money, whereas child D is, and so on.

A redundancy principle operates in family life, in that a family will tend to interact in repetitive sequences in all areas of its life. That is, the entire system can be run by a relatively small set of rules governing relationships. Consider the rules that define the following relationship between husband and wife as they prepare to go out for the evening with another couple:

w: I wish you would update your dress. I'd really appreciate it if you'd pay greater attention to what you wear. Why don't you buy yourself a new suit?
H: I just couldn't buy new clothes for myself when you and the kids need so many things.
w: But we want you to do things for yourself too.
H: I just couldn't put myself before you all.

Contrary to initial appearances, the overt one-down behavior of the husband (wherein he places his needs "one-down" from those of the rest of the family) is quite controlling. What sort of family rule have they worked out? The wife is allowed to complain about her husband's appearance, but he retains control over the family's expenditure of money. He apparently does not intend to follow her suggestion and, moreover, cannot be faulted because he is the good person sacrificing for his family (and likely contributes to their feeling guilty). This couple is caught up in a repetitive exchange that defines and redefines the nature of their relationship. The fact is that they execute no action and so eliminate the possibility of finding new solutions to their differences (Goldenberg & Goldenberg, 1980).

The concept of "role" held by the MRI strategy is different from that commonly held. Jackson (1977) observed that the common usage of role is from an individually-oriented perspective which deemphasizes the interaction among family members. Jackson further observed that role is commonly tied to stereotypes created by cultural and theoretical viewpoints. In contrast, the MRI perspective relative to family roles is that they are always an artifact of the ongoing interactions among family members. It is the family's rules that govern their interactions which create roles.

GALOIS' MATHEMATICAL GROUP THEORY AND THE GAME WITHOUT END

Families with problems frequently attempt many extraordinary measures to bring about change, and in spite of these generally well-intentioned efforts, the problems remain and often become even worse. Additionally, in the mental health community, there have been numerous pages written addressing the problem of assisting "resistant" clients who, despite the equally extraordinary efforts of well-intentioned therapists, seem to remain the same. In considering this dilemma, the MRI strategy posits that persistence and change must be considered together. Thus in observing a problem, the first question to ask is "How does this undesirable situation persist?" with a second question to follow "What is required to change it?" (Watzlawick, Weakland, & Fisch, 1974).

The MRI strategy has utilized Galois' mathematic group theory as an "exemplificatory" analogy to explain how problems persist. Galois, a French mathematician who lived in the early nineteenth century, defined a mathematical group as an entity composed of members that are all alike in one common characteristic. Galois proposed that a group has four properties:

1. All members of the group have a common denominator and the outcome of any combination of two or more members is itself a member of the group. For example: "The constitution of an imaginary country provides for unlimited parliamentary debate. The rule can be used to paralyze democratic procedure completely—the opposition party only has to engage in endless speeches to make impossible any decision that is not to its liking. To escape this impass, a change of the rule is absolutely necessary, but can be made impossible precisely by what is to be changed, i.e., by endless filibuster" (Watzlawick, Weakland, & Fisch, 1974, p. 15). A family illustration might be one wherein the family is dominated by a tyrannical mother and the family rule (the common denominator) is "whatever you do, don't upset Mother!" Any sign of anger by the mother creates great anxiety in family members, which is calmed only when the mother is no longer upset. Thus family members may behave in many different ways, but all will always be aware of the mother's reaction to what they do. Intense group pressure will also be brought to bear on any member who "upsets" the mother and will continue until the offender changes to please the family matriarch.

2. Members of the group may be combined in varying sequences, yet the outcome of the combination remains the same. For example: "When a teenager's delinquent behavior improves, his parents may discover delinquent behavior in a child previously regarded as the 'good one' " (Watzlawick, Weakland, & Fisch, 1974, p. 16). From a purely

systemic perspective, this is an example of homeostasis whereby members of a family may change roles, but their basic overall interaction remains the same.

3. Each group will have an identity member who when combined with any other member number will result in no change. (An example of this will follow).

4. Any group member combined with his/her reciprocal or opposite will give the identity number. For example: "light and dark, figure and ground, good and evil, past and future, and many other such pairs are merely the complementary aspects of one and the same reality or frame of reference, their seemingly incompatible and mutually exclusive nature notwithstanding" (Watzlawick, Weakland, & Fisch, 1974, p. 18). Another example: "One of the common fallacies about change is the conclusion that if something is bad, its opposite must of necessity be good. The woman who divorces a weak man in order to marry a strong one often discovers to her dismay that while her second marriage should be the exact opposite of the first, nothing much has actually changed" (Watzlawick, Weakland, & Fisch, 1974, p. 20). In the latter example, the identity member would be the woman's behavior in intimate relationships, ultimately leading to dissatisfaction no matter the strength or weakness of her partner.

In each of the preceding examples, dramatic internal changes can occur with a system (group) and still the system remains the same. Within the MRI strategy such changes are called *first-order changes*. The MRI strategy asserts that all systems are trapped by the rules that ensure the continuance of the system. Those rules governing the system are generally uncomprehended by its members. In families, the set of rules governing its members are generally accepted as unquestioned "common sense." A system that runs through many internal "first-order" changes without changing the basic rules which govern the system is said to be caught in a *game without end*. Such a system "cannot generate from within itself the conditions for its own change; it cannot produce the rules for changing its own rules" (Watzlawick, Weakland, & Fisch, 1974), p. 22).

Change of the rules that govern the system is called *second-order change*. Such changes do occur as everyday phenomena. However, as suggested by Watzlawick et al. (1974):

> The occurrence of second-order change is ordinarily viewed as something uncontrollable, even incomprehensible, a quantum jump, a sudden illum-

ination which unpredictably came at the end of long, often frustrating mental and emotional labor, sometimes almost as an act of grace in the theological sense. (p. 23)

Therapeutic change emanating from the MRI strategy is brought about by disrupting the sequence of first-order changes (the game without end) by which a family has attempted to correct its problem and in a sense forces the family to violate the rules that have governed its actions. This violation forces the family to generate new rules in order to maintain the integrity of the family system and thus, second-order change occurs.

PROBLEM-SOLUTION INTERACTION

What happens when a family needs to change or modify its rules? As children grow, they press for redefinitions of family relationships. They no longer wish to accompany their parents on weekends, preferring to be with friends. They expect to be given allowances to spend as they wish, to decide for themselves a suitable bedtime, to listen to music which may be repellent to their parents' ears. They want to borrow the family car, sleep over at a friend's house, pursue interests alien to those traditionally cared about in the family. They challenge family values and traditions, they no longer share their innermost thoughts with parents, they insist on being treated as equals. All of this contributes to disequilibrium within the family system, a sense of loss, and perhaps a feeling of strangeness until new interactional patterns restore family balance (Goldenberg & Goldenberg, 1980).

The MRI strategy posits that problems develop through the mishandling of normal life difficulties such as those suggested in the preceding paragraph. Difficulties are viewed as probable occurrances in the course of a family's lifetime and include accidents, loss of work, and transitions in individual and family life cycles such as marriage, the birth of a child, children leaving home, and the like. For a difficulty to become a "Problem" (with a capital "P"), that difficulty is exacerbated by the overemphasis or underemphasis (exaggeration or denial) that so often characterize the attempted solutions by means of which people inadvertently prolong and elaborate their problems. Watzlawick et al. (1974) describe the single, overarching principle of problem formation as being the persistence of the participants in continuing to attempt a solution despite available evidence that it is precisely what is *not* working. This tendency to become mired in attempting *more of the same* already demonstrated unsuccessful solution is what converts the *solution* into the *problem* by creating said problem through the mishandling (inappropriate attempted solution) of what was previously a mere *difficulty* (Bodin, 1981). Thus, for a difficulty to become a problem, two conditions must be met: (1) The difficulty is mishandled, and (2) when the difficulty is not resolved, more of the same "solution" is applied. The original difficulty becomes escalated by a vicious-cycle process into a problem whose eventual size and nature may have little apparent similarity to the original difficulty (Fisch, Weakland, & Segal, 1982).

When families encounter difficulties in their lives, they attempt to deal with them in ways which are consistent with their context and frame of reference. Their "attempted solutions" are maintained because they are considered logical, necessary, or the "only thing to do." Three major ways by which difficulties might be mishandled have been dominant within the MRI strategy:

1. Action is necessary but is not taken.
2. Action is taken when it should not be.
3. Action is taken at the wrong level.

These three types of mishandling have been detailed by Watzlawick et al. (1974). They described the first type of mishandling:

> One way of mishandling a problem is to behave as if it did not exist. For this form of denial, we have borrowed the term *terrible simplification*. Two consequences follow from it: (a) acknowledgement, let alone any attempted solution of the problem is seen as a manifestation of madness or badness; and (b) the problem requiring change becomes greatly compounded by the "problems" created through its mishandling. (p. 46)

The second type of mishandling has as its premise the refusal to accept any proposed solution other than one based on a Utopian belief that things *should be* a certain way, thus precluding more modest and attainable goals by insisting on the impossible and making a "federal case" out of the fact of its unattainability. This type of problem formation based on exaggeration is frequently self-evident except to those sharing the particular underlying Utopian belief. Denial and exaggeration of difficulties (underemphasis and overemphasis) are thus types of mishandling which, though apparently opposites, are alike in presenting *extremist* types of proposed solutions.

The third type of mishandling described by Watzlawick et al. (1974) has "paradox" as its theme: that unresolvability of various difficulties without the introduction of *second-order change* which transcends the level containing the contradictions of the paradox. Put more simply, the usually stated quid pro quo originally underlying the relationship may need revision, but the relationship contains no rules which allow its participants to acknowledge, agree upon, nor adopt the necessary revisions. Thus, a command to be spontaneous, for example, is a paradox that requires another level of analysis, perhaps stemming from outside intervention, to envision and effect the second-order change essential to resolving the problem promoted by the paradox.

RECURSIVE COMPLEMENTARITIES

The previous pages describe the evolution of Rational Emotive Family Therapy in addressing the multiple communications of stability, change, and the meaningful new as follows: (1) stable requests for the Rational-Emotive position as a foundation; (2) change requests to employ the Rational-Emotive position from within a family systems perspective; and (3) the meaningful new in the form of the MRI strategy as a theory of change that equally and conceptually complements each distinction. Merely integrating the Rational-Emotive position with a family systems perspective makes as much sense as pouring white and red wine into the same glass—the result is a pallid mixture that loses the essence of both. On the other hand, we do not have to choose between a theory of persons and a theory of persons in relationship. Keeney and Ross (1985) fully frame how the MRI strategy offers both the wide angle lens of an interactional view with the ability to use the magnifying glass of individual cognitions simultaneously. They further present two specific recursive complementarities.

Keeney and Ross posited that the first recursive complementarity in utilizing the MRI strategy is one between problem behavior and problem-solving behavior. They refer to Watzlawick and his colleagues' summarization of this relationship: "the solution is the problem." "The relationship between a problem and efforts to solve it are recursively intertwined: the problem arises out of efforts to solve it while attempted solutions arise from experiencing the problem" (Keeney & Ross, 1985, p. 88).

For example Fisch, Weakland, & Segal (1982) present a case wherein a woman's concern about her sexual performance, which she had previously found satisfying, developed into a problem following a conversation with several of her female friends. During the conversation she began to wonder whether she had ever had an orgasm. Since her friends' descriptions of orgasm differed from her own sexual experience, she concluded that she had not had an orgasm and set out to achieve one. That decision turned her sex life into a problem. She no longer found sex enjoyable because, in her own words, "I kept, you know, waiting for this other to happen, or at one point it was so scientific that, you know, it was like there was no pleasure." Her efforts to solve what she perceived as a difficulty created an even greater "problem" for her.

It follows that a practical solution for this woman might involve blocking her attempts to solve the problem. Although blocking the problem in order to eradicate the need for a solution would be the "common sense" tact, the MRI strategy shows how blocking a solution eradicates the problem. Thus, problems are conceptualized as half of a more encompassing recursive complementarity that necessarily includes solutions.

Keeney and Ross posit that the other complementarity within the MRI strategy involves the relationship between behavior and cognition. They refer to Watzlawick and his colleagues' use of the term "frame" to speak about the way humans perceive, conceptualize, understand, and experience a situation. One task in seeking change therefore is to alter the cognitive frames which organize behavior. This change of frame is called a "reframe" and is defined by them as altering the conceptual, emotional, and/or perceptual view of a situation so that the same "facts" take on an entirely different meaning.

The MRI strategy thus asserts the construction of two recursive complementarities. The first is that between problem behavior and behavioral efforts to solve the problem. The second involves a higher order distinction between behavior and the cognitive frame, or between what Bateson (1972; 1979) has referred to as a simple action and punctuation of a context. Using these recursive complementarities, Rational-Emotive Family Therapy (REFT) is able to organize patterns of systemic therapeutic intervention.

THE ABCs OF REFT

REFT proposes that whenever family members are engaged in unsuccessful problem–solution interactions, they are experiencing disturbed

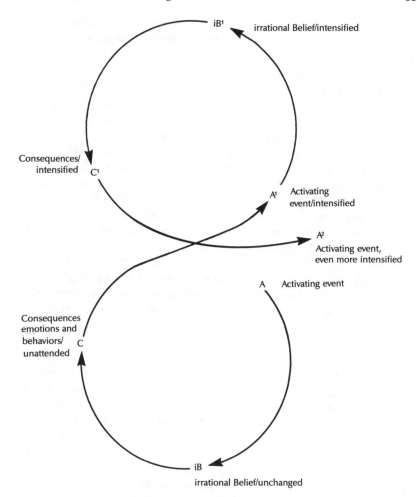

FIGURE 3.1   Deviation-amplification illustrated by not seeking to change the irrational Belief (iB) thus leaving emotions and behaviors (C) unattended contributing to "more-of-the-same-only-worse" problem-solution interactions.

emotions and/or behaviors at point C (emotional and/or behavioral consequences; *the unsuccessful solution*). C is hypothesized to be preceded by A (activating experience or event; *the problem*). This represents the recursive complementarity between the problem and efforts to solve the problem. To change the organization of this relation requires addressing the cognitive frame that gives it meaning. This is the B (belief). REFT advocates therapeutic intervention that attempts to change the B in order to break up the pattern of logic connecting the problem (A) and the unsuccessful solution (C). When that pattern is broken, the problem–solution relation is disconnected with the practical effect of eradicating the problem (and solution). The latter is that second recursive complementarity of a higher order distinction between the problem and family members' belief (i.e., evaluation) about it.

For example, were a husband to be thinking that his wife did not show him enough gestures of affection on a daily basis at A (the problem), he could experience either predominantly rational Beliefs (rBs) or irrational Beliefs (iBs) at B. Rational beliefs at B might take the form of desires—wants, wishes, preferences—that his wife show him more affection. These rBs would almost invariably contribute to his experiencing consequences at C relative to the context, such as feeling sorrow, regret, and frustration. These feelings, however, are not those that would paralyze his problem-solving efforts and thus his actions at C would likely be such that he would be open to considering alternatives if his initial solutions were unsuccessful. He would not tend to get stuck in a singular class of solution. Desiring at B, he would likely be thinking thoughts such as "It's sad I've not succeeded in getting my wife to show me more affection yet. Perhaps there are other ways which I might try."

By contrast, were this husband to experience irrational Beliefs (iBs) along the lines of "How awful it is that my wife won't show me the affection I must have. I can't stand failing in getting her to do so. I must be pretty inadequate!" These iBs would tend to contribute to his experiencing at C feelings of severe depression, low frustration tolerance, and self-deprecation. Also, at C, his actions would tend to be quite dysfunctional relative to adaptively dealing with the problem—passively giving up efforts to explore alternative solutions, self-pity acts à la alcoholism to promote his wife's affection, and the like.

REFT posits that when consequences, such as in the above illustration, at C are left unattended (by not seeking to change the B), they feed back to the problem at A in a deviation-amplifying manner. The resulting interactions become a vicious cycle of "more-of-the-same-only-worse" problem–solution interactions. This process is illustrated in Figure 3.1. While understanding that changing either A, B, or C would effect change in the other two, REFT makes a therapeutic distinction in selecting B as the focus for intervention. Chapters in the upcoming section will now expound upon the therapeutic implications of REFT.

Part II
Therapeutic Implications

"REFT is not merely a 'talk therapy.' Once a more rational belief is confimed, then enactment of alternative behavioral solution sequences become the next strategic change process."

4

Therapist Distinctions

Minuchin (1974) observed the following relative to family functioning:

A family is subject to inner pressure coming from developmental changes
in its own members and subsystems and to outer pressure coming from
demands to accommodate to the significant social institutions that have
an impact on family members. Responding to these demands from both
within and without requires a constant transformation of the position of
family members in relation to one another. (p. 60)

The development and maintenance of both a more rational self-in-
context and a more rational context-around-self are the major aims of
Rational-Emotive Family Therapy (REFT). Rational is not meant to have
any fixed definition, although in a general sense it would be understood
to be that which aids and abets goal attainment and life satisfaction.
This is seen as the task of life: to blend the diversity of individual growth
with the unity of family group membership in ways that contribute to
goal attainment and life satisfaction. For this to occur, the varieties of
individual, self-actualizing functioning need to balance with the
varieties of the family system as it adjusts to the continually changing
demands of its own environmental context. Facilitating this evolutionary
balance is the task of the REFT therapist.

In beginning any therapeutic effort, the therapist sets certain
guidelines for what distinctions will be used to organize it. This normally means which questions are to be addressed and which ones ig-
nored. In beginning REFT, the therapist seeks to view therapy in
cybernetic terms: unsuccessful solutions and problems are connected
through a feedback relationship wherein the more one tries to solve
a problem the more one maintains it. Problems and solutions express

a complementary relationship that defines a cybernetic system. Problems are stabilized by changing the solutions that have been unsuccessful in solving them (Keeney & Ross, 1983). The REFT therapist facilitates this process by drawing certain distinctions that contribute to identifying "the meaningful new" for family members in order that they might reorganize the way they organize themselves. These distinctions involve ideas about being a cybernetic therapist, rational and irrational family functioning, invested "holons," sequences, facilitating more rational family functioning, and expanding the ABCs of REFT.

THE CYBERNETIC THERAPIST

Pask (1969) differentiated two types of goal directed systems—"taciturn systems" and "language oriented systems." He defined them in stating:

> Taciturn systems are those for which the observer asserts or discovers the goal (purpose in), which is thereafter equated with the purpose *for* the systems in question. In contrast, language oriented systems can be asked or instructed to *adopt* goals by anyone who knows the object language and they may state and describe their own goals, using the same medium. (p. 25)

Taciturn systems allow an observer to act as though he or she is distinct from the system of interest. Toasters, radios, and televisions, for example, can be seen as having a particular purpose of operation. The higher order of recursion that involved a human prescribing a goal for the machine is conveniently forgotten. For the most part, any ongoing interaction between operator and machine is overlooked. At this order of purpose, any "circuit" that connects human and machine tends to be disregarded. Occasionally, however, their connection is highlighted (e.g., the human operator gets an electrical shock from the device).

In language-oriented systems, the observer more clearly enters the system by defining and requesting *his or her* purpose. This is a higher order of purpose in that the achievement of the system's goal requires that the observer do more than just push a button to start a machine. Whereas persons are not seen as contributing much to toasting toast (other than pushing the lever), computer operators are more readily seen as part of the system which computes. Once the computer is turned on, the operator must continually interact with it to achieve a goal.

Family therapists have traditionally encountered families as either taciturn or language oriented systems. The former stance views the family system as a black box that can be observed and operated on from an outside position. The latter brings the therapist into the system, prohibiting any disconnection of the therapist–family "circuit."

The REFT therapist as a cybernetic therapist needs several basic skills: an ability to be flexible in his or her actions and an ability to discern and then use the effects of those actions to direct subsequent actions. These skills correspond to the ways the therapist operates as a "receptor," "analyzer," and "effector." The task of creating difference concerns the therapist operating as "effector," whereas discerning difference concerns the therapist operating as "receptor/analyzer." When the relationship between effector and receptor/analyzer, or intervention and assessment, is recursively organized, it may be seen as a cybernetic system (Keeney, 1983).

Generally stated, any problematic system requires three ingredients for correction. First, a sufficient range of sensors and analyzers to detect difference. Second, a sufficient range of varied actions to facilitate the creation of difference. And finally, and most importantly, the system must be able to recursively link sensors and analyzers with effectors so as to provide self-correction. The REFT therapist's task is to enter a family system in a way that connects their sensors and analyzers with their effectors as recursive parts of self-corrective feedback (Keeney, 1983). This process is the ABCDEF of REFT (the "DEF" to be presented later in this chapter).

More specifically, REFT therapists maintain an interactive, facilitative style. Because they grasp the importance of identifying and altering irrational beliefs and the value of rational beliefs, they are alert and watchful for specific cues to these beliefs. Key words, phrases, intonations, and nonverbal emotional and behavioral interactions among family members represent cues to which the REFT therapist seeks to attend. Thus, the REFT therapist avoids asking overly general open-ended questions that family members might respond to with prolonged rambling. Instead, the REFT therapist seeks to ask direct, specific questions so that the interaction is more a dialogue than a family monologue, with the therapist carefully following up on words and concepts revealed in the resulting interaction. The therapist acts as receptor/analyzer/effector to facilitate feedback to keep the system in pursuit of its therapeutic purpose.

Walen et al. (1980) offered an important caution for the REFT therapist—"the Advice Trap," wherein the therapist either gives family members solutions to their problems or appears to be recommending a particular solution. The REFT therapist as cybernetic therapist first facilitates family members' rational thinking in seeking options and alternatives. The therapist then aids family members in learning adaptive problem-solving methods, methods characterized by helpful as opposed to hurtful emotions and behaviors.

RATIONAL AND IRRATIONAL FAMILY FUNCTIONING

Living systems such as families are composed of "dissipative structures," that is, of structures that are not simply in a permanent steady state, as are structures of crystal. The structures of living systems must always be in some state of flux and are in that way able to achieve new orders of complexity and new levels of adaptive organization. Old structures dissipate and in the flux of their dissipation are replaced by new ones. Under the evolutionary demands of the surrounding environment, these new structures will also disappear (Glansdorff & Prigogine, 1971). Minuchin and Fishman (1981) noted the importance of family systems' ability to maintain themselves, but emphasized equally a system's ability to transform itself, to reach new states of complexity and adaptive differentiation of structure.

REFT, in incorporating the MRI theory of change, accordingly accepts the notion that problems develop through the mishandling of difficulties that occur in the course of a family's lifetime. Said difficulties turn into "Problems" (with a capital "P" suggesting perceived insolubility) when a difficulty is mishandled, and then when not resolved, more of the same "solution" is applied. While it may be tempting to assume that a rationally-functioning family solves all of its problems, the REFT therapist takes the view that it encounters problems which may persist, but does not become paralyzed by "more of the same" solutions. Such families seek to address their problems through discussion, which may become heated at times. The heated discussions that occur in rationally-functioning families, however, are seen by the REFT therapist as "good arguments"; a good argument being one that contributes to getting the matter settled and leaves family members feeling closer together afterwards rather than farther apart (Bodin, 1981). Problems are dealt with in these families in any way that works for smooth operation of the family; these could include the invocation of reasonably stable rules for first-order changes or higher level "meta-rules" that allow for changes in the present rules and thus second-order change without having to resort to symptom development.

The inevitability of change is recognized by the REFT therapist. Those who study family development have asserted that all families go through phases in their family life and that transitions between phases are frequently experienced as "crises." While there are some families whose entire life cycle seems to be an uninterrupted series of disasters, these families are relatively rare. More likely, most family crises are tied rather specifically to the tasks required to make the transition from one phase to the next. Thus, the childless couple who experience contentment may face considerable marital stress with the birth of a baby, contributing to changes in roles, freedom of movement, economic status, and so on. Another set of parents may do an excellent job when nurturing is needed, but fail miserably and see their smoothly functioning family system disrupted when their child begins to move out from the confining boundaries of the family unit, as when he or she enters school. Another example of a critical transition within a family might occur when one or both parents have enjoyed being playful with their child, a "pal," but have significant difficulty taking on the role of adult models, offering leadership and guidance when the child reaches adolescence and such new parental action is called for.

Each transitional crisis tends to call for new styles of coping by all family members. While regression to less effective solutions is always a possible accompanying danger to the transitional stress, the crisis also presents the family with an opportunity to grow by learning more effective coping strategies (Goldenberg & Goldenberg, 1980). Consider the following case illustration:

A domineering, stubborn husband; his meek, child-like wife; and their 16-year-old daughter Joyce were approaching the point in Joyce's therapy in which they were becoming aware that the 16-year-old's repeated behavior of running away and sexually acting-out often occurred after father and daughter had had a particularly intense encounter with one another. In their encounters each usually tried to convince the other of the "rightness" of his or her view by means of shouting arguments. When all three came to the therapist's office after a crisis phone call, they began by relating that two days ago Joyce had met a former boyfriend and spent the night with him at the beach without letting her parents know where she was, and had been "raped" by him. The next morning, i.e., yesterday, Joyce had come home sobbing to tell her parents of the outrage that had befallen her. The father was incensed. He didn't believe Joyce's cry of rape; he accused her of being a slut. Predictably, this triggered Joyce, and the father and daughter entered a shouting match. The meek wife spoke up, addressing her husband, "Why object now, it's happened many times before. I don't like it either; but I like it even less that she is getting between you and me again. I had begun to think recently that maybe I was more to you than just the 'child-mother' of your daughter. I don't want her to ruin that." (McPherson, Brackelmanns, & Newman, 1974, p. 83)

A new, more rational belief and with it, a new alternative "solution" has been introduced.

Such life events all call for some change on the part of a family and its members by bringing with them increased pressure and disorganization. This occurs because many of the patterns and regularities that have developed up to this point are disrupted by the new experience; they must be reorganized if the family is to adaptively evolve in its development. In the broader sense, the continuing life task for the rationally-functioning family is to balance stability and change so that the family as a whole and its individual members can evolve, without either becoming "stuck" or being overwhelmed by sudden, drastic changes.

It follows then that irrational family functioning connotes a marked and persistent failure to negotiate these stresses in a rational way. "The label of pathology *(Authors' note: irrationality)* would be reserved for families who in the face of stress increase the *rigidity of their transactional patterns . . .* and avoid or resist any exploration of alternatives" (Minuchin, 1974, p. 60). When a family is rationally-functioning, it adapts to the inevitable stresses of life in a way which preserves family continuity while facilitating reorganization. When, however, a family reacts with pathological rigidity, irrationality characterizes its functioning.

As discussed in Chapter 2, the Rational-Emotive position is characterized by its stressing the contribution of cognition in alleviating symptomatology in the therapeutic milieu. The REFT therapist similarly stresses the contribution of cognition in the family therapy setting. More specifically, in working within an REFT framework, the REFT therapist focuses on those beliefs (B) that give meaning to the problem (A) and then contribute to the unsuccessful solutions (C) the family has attempted. Those beliefs come in two major forms, rational beliefs and irrational beliefs. It is important to remember that both rational and irrational beliefs are *evaluations*, that indicate a sense of personal significance. They are not definitions, descriptions or interpretations (see discussion of Wessler and Wessler's 8-step model in Chapter 2). Thus, rational and irrational beliefs are not merely sentences describing problems such as "Our family is in turmoil and we're at a loss as to what to do about it"; rather they express an evaluation of such descriptions of family circumstances (e.g., rational: "This is troubling and we need assistance"; irrational: "This is horrible and nothing is going to change things.")

The following criteria adapted from Walen et al. (1980) tend to characterize those beliefs that lead to more rational family functioning. Examine the following rational belief, "It would be bad if we had to move to another city," against each criterion.

1. *The belief adequately considers the context.* The belief takes into account the context of the problem–solution interaction. In so doing, it is internally and externally consistent. Considering the example above, certain unpleasant effects would likely occur anytime a move is made. Presumably, familiar friends and places would be left behind and there would be a degree of sadness experienced in that parting.

2. *The belief is relative or conditional.* It is not absolutistic. A belief leading to more rational family functioning is normally stated as a want, wish, hope, or preference, and therefore reflects a desiring, rather than a demanding philosophy. In regard to the above example, the implication is "We'd prefer to stay where we are" (not "We must absolutely!").

3. *The belief results in emotional moderation.* Beliefs which contribute to more rational family functioning lead to feelings that may range from mild to strong, depending on the context of the problem–solution interaction. This is an important distinction, since a common misconception about the Rational–Emotive position is that rational thinking leads to the absence of emotion. Quite the contrary; it would be foolish to assume that a zero level of emotional concern would contribute to attaining goals and experiencing life satisfaction. Moderate emotional arousal serves as a motivation to seeking new alternative solutions to problems while underarousal or overarousal is clearly a hindrance to doing so. Returning to the above example, when the family members think about moving, they likely feel sad but not depressed into immobility.

4. *The belief reflects openness to new experience.* Thus, beliefs leading to more rational family functioning allow for the freedom to pursue new alternative solutions to problems in a less fearful manner. It also follows that the risks involved in doing "something different" are accepted as part of the price to pay for goal attainment. Back to the example, while

some loss and sadness might be involved in the move, there is also the implication that this is not enough to prevent consideration and exploration of the potentials offered in moving to another city. There is an openness to new experience.

Beliefs that contribute to irrational family functioning, by contrast, tend to be characterized by different features.

1. *The belief does not adequately consider the context.* Such beliefs tend to be extreme evaluative underestimations or exaggerations and are often reflected in descriptors such as "awful," "terrible," or "horrible." An example of such a belief might be "It would be just horrible if we had to move. We just couldn't stand it." Such a belief obviously does not adequately consider that the new location would offer many of the amenities of the present situation, or possibly more. Further, it is unlikely that the family's present living arrangements are perfect in all respects.

2. *The belief is a command.* As such, it represents an absolutistic rather than relativistic philosophy and is expressed as demands (versus desires). Other absolutistic descriptors include "must" (versus "it would be better"), "need" (versus "want"), and "have to" (versus "prefer"). Relative to problem–solution interactions in families, such beliefs are often presented in a contradictory manner (e.g., parents simultaneously demand that their children obey their requests to do distasteful chores and like what they're doing!) To return to the irrational example above, the implied command is clearly "We must not move!"

3. *The belief contributes to disturbed emotional experience.* Apathy or severe anxiety can be debilitating at worst and nonproductive at best. If a problem–solution interaction is at a "more of the same" stalemate and family members are thinking "It doesn't matter. . ." or "It's just awful. . ." they will most likely experience one of the two nonhelpful emotional extremes, apathy or severe anxiety. Returning to the irrational example, were family members to think that moving didn't matter at all, their apathy would surely make matters worse. Likewise, severe anxiety in viewing a move as "awful" would tend to similarly cripple their problem–solving interaction.

4. *The belief reflects a rigidity relative to new experience.* When family members are tied up in absolutes and shackled by disturbing emotions, their openness to new alternative problem–solution interactions will tend to be minimal.

THE INVESTED HOLON

Only a small percentage of families seek therapeutic assistance by specifically requesting relationship therapy. While this may change as public awareness of family therapy as a treatment entity increases, typically one marital partner or family member seeks an appointment. While it is usually preferable to physically convene all involved family members, this is simply not always practical or possible. In such instances, the REFT therapist then seeks to work with the *invested holon*.

In discussing the evolution of a family system, Minuchin and Fishman following Koestler (1979) introduced the term *holon* to describe entities that are simultaneously a whole unto themselves and a part of some other superordinate whole. Koestler's term is based on the Greek *holos* (whole) with the suffix *on*, suggesting a particle or part, as in *proton*. Minuchin and Fishman described the term *holon* stating:

> Every holon—the individual, the nuclear family, the extended family, and the community—is both a whole and a part, not more one than the other. A holon exerts competitive energy for autonomy and self-preservation as a whole. It also carries integrative energy as a part. The nuclear family is a holon of the extended family, the extended family of the community, and so on. Each whole contains the part, and each part also contains the "program" that the whole imposes. Part and whole contain each other in a continuing, current, and ongoing process of communication and interrelationship. (p. 13)

The individual as a holon, for example, developing in context, incorporates the concepts of self-in-context and context-around-self. Individual family members influence the family system and yet are influenced by it in constantly recurring sequences of interaction. There are three important points herein for the REFT therapist. In positing the individual as a holon, REFT accords individual members' activities the power to alter the superordinate family's interactions. This is in accordance with a truly cybernetic model. Second, the individual as a holon also suggests further compatibility with a family-systems perspective in that individual family members are viewed as continually involved in reciprocities with the larger family system, each influencing the other through a circular model of cause and effect. Third, REFT asserts that the internal experience of individual family members changes as the family system in which they live changes and likewise, the family system changes as the internal experience of individual family members changes.

When family therapy was young, individual therapy was the dominant model of treatment for psychological ills. Family therapy was initially seen as simply another method to treat the individual client. Once it became understood that family therapy was not a method but rather a conceptual orientation to clinical problems, the dichotomy between individual and family therapy dissolved. From a family therapy perspective, all psychological treatment is the treatment of families (systems). This is the case whether one, two, or all family members are physically present in the therapy room. What the REFT therapist thinks about problems and how to treat them is more important than how many family members might be in the room. REFT is no less family-systems oriented because it advocates doing therapy at times when fewer than the total family are physically present.

REFT therapists look at individual family members, subsystems within the family (e.g., marital: consisting of the husband and wife), and the family as a whole as holons. They are each a whole unto themselves and simultaneously a part of a larger whole. Because they do, REFT therapists recognize that intervention at the level of the holon will impact total family functioning whether that holon is one individual family member, a subsystem, or the total family group. It is not any holon, however, that the REFT therapist seeks to work with when it is not possible (e.g., a spouse or other family member flatly refuses to participate) or, for some specific reason not appropriate (e.g., an infant or small child whose attention span disrupts rather than contributes to the process), to physically convene all involved family members. Rather, it is that holon who has "invested" in therapy who represents the physically convened treatment unit in such instances.

The REFT therapist very early in the therapy process seeks to determine which family member or members are "invested" in pursuing treatment—the holon most committed to change. Ideally, the member or members identified as the "invested holon" will communicate the following: (1) I have a problem, (2) I've tried to solve it and have been unsuccessful, and (3) I am requesting your assistance (Segal & Kahn, 1986). The invested holon will not necessarily include the identified patient. Since REFT utilizes an interpersonal systems model, the therapist can facilitate change in the behavior of the identified patient by assisting the patient's intimates to change their problem-solving behavior.

An analogy to offer further explanation in this regard was provided by Fisch et al. (1982). They viewed an undesirable family interaction as an observed tennis rally. If one wished to end it as rapidly as possible, it would only require that one player not return the ball. The intervener's effectiveness would be reduced if he or she were limited to influencing only one particular player, especially if that player was less interested in ending the rally. However, the intervener's effectiveness would also be reduced if he or she were required to get both players to lay down their racquets simultaneously. Obviously, the intervener's greatest maneuverability and effectiveness lies in having the option to decide whether one or both players needed to be influenced and, if only one player, which of the two could more easily be influenced to end the rally.

Some beginning REFT therapists have questioned REFT's family or systems orientation if the physical treatment unit at times did not include the identified patient. Possibly the most critical part of their training has been understanding that REFT is a conceptual framework; what matters is how the process is viewed, not whether sessions are convened with only one, or two, or all family members physically present. There are many "family therapists" who hold sessions in which a total family might be physically present, but conceive the problem in purely individual terms, not interactional at all. While they may hold "family" sessions, the therapy is basically individual treatment.

The REFT therapist is principally concerned with the interaction which revolves around the presenting complaint (the A), keeping in mind that the overriding goal is to alter the belief (the B), and with that, the problem-maintaining emotions and behaviors (the C) of all those family members participating in it. Consistent with that interactional view, it is assumed that altering the B and the C of the invested holon, be it comprised of an individual family member, a couple, or some combination of members, can influence the beliefs, emotions, and behaviors of the physically absent members of the family. For the most part, problem-maintaining interactions are seen as representing a positive feedback, deviation-amplifying loop. That is, the identified patient's actions invite solution-attempting reactions on the part of the invested holon, but these solution-attempting reactions have only escalated the identified patient's deviant actions, which, in turn, invites stronger efforts, and so on. Seen as a loop, this cycle can be interrupted if the input of either the invested holon or the identified patient or both is altered.

For the REFT therapist confronted by difficulties in physically convening all involved family members, the important question to consider is "Who in the family is most interested in resolving the problem?" This is likely to be that holon most discomforted by the problem. In most child-centered complaints, for example, the invested holon is not likely to be the identified patient—the child. More probable, the greater discomfort is being experienced by the parents. They represent the holon who will respond affirmatively to (1) "So you see your child's misbehavior as a problem for the both of you. . . "; (2) "You've been unsuccessful in deciding how to rectify the problem."

SEQUENCES

"Problems" and "solutions" are not the names of simple action; rather, they are names of categories of interaction. If a husband complains that his wife is "depressed," what specific actions are classified by that category of interaction? Can the husband clearly mark when the depression begins and when it ends? When depression or any category of interaction is analyzed, it is found to refer to a *sequence* of actions in some social context (Keeney & Ross, 1985).

   In general, any reference to problems and solutions suggests underlying sequences of simple actions. Since these sequences are organized in a way that can lead to either discomfort and pain, or comfort and relief, they are named "problems" and "attempted solutions." The focus for the REFT therapist is addressing the organization of a whole sequence, not only one particular part, whether that part be distinguished by simple actions such as looking sad or yelling out in anger, or classes of interaction such as problems and solutions. The REFT therapist does not aim to change problems or solutions alone, but instead to alter the pattern of interaction between them. For this to occur, the therapist must have a clear understanding of sequences and be able to readily "see" them.

   A sequence has no particular status as a psychological construct; it is simply a word used to designate a collection of interpersonal actions that, taken as a cybernetic whole, constitute a dynamic entity that regularly appears in a family's life process (Umbarger, 1983). In seeking to "see" sequences, the REFT therapist takes a stance wherein he or she retires from active participation with the family in order to observe the ritual exchanges among family members. To see sequences, the therapist needs to assume this role of observer, and also at times, the role of director of the family's drama. The development of this observational skill is essential in seeing and sensing routine sequences of family action. The viewing of video tapes of sessions is often of great help in acquiring this skill.

In addition to this general stance, Umbarger (1983) outlined several specific tips which indicate when one is face-to-face with a sequence. These include:

1. When a sequence is concluded, punctuated by the family itself (before taking another interactional breath), the therapist can experience this pause as a moment of transactional blankness, a time when it seems things have ended and nothing else has begun. The family may be quiet, frozen, emotionally stricken, or even obviously finished, perhaps punctuating the conclusion of the sequence by complaining, "This is how it always turns out!"
2. The therapist recognizes the outcome of the sequence before it actually arrives. It's a story that he or she has heard the family tell before.
3. A cogent comment expressed by the therapist is assimilated by the family in such a way that even the therapist forgets the remark.
4. A variation of the "lost remark": When a sequence has not yet run through its cycle, efforts by the therapist to intervene will be for naught. The family will override the intrusion (unless it is very strong), thereby alerting the therapist that a sequence is in progress.
5. Valuable clues to the steps in a sequence can be gotten by the therapist asking the family to describe how things unfold by noting who says what to whom, who responds next, what happens then, etc.

In addition to being a good observer and mastering such tip-offs, the REFT therapist should also seek to develop a scenario of sequences that fits common family interactions as adequately as possible and not wait for confirmation that the details of the scenario are absolutely correct. These scenarios may be large or small. Haley (1976) offered a number of excellent examples of such scenarios describing routine family interactions. One example involves the problem–solution interaction of two parents and their child:

1. One parent, usually the mother, is in an intense relationship with the child. The mother attempts to deal with the child's symptomatic behavior with a mixture of affection and exasperation.
2. The child's symptomatic behavior becomes even more extreme.
3. The mother calls on the father for assistance in resolving the problem.

4. The father steps in to take charge and deal with the child.
5. The mother reacts against the father, insisting that he is not dealing with the situation properly.
6. The father withdraws, giving up his attempt to resolve the problem.
7. The mother deals with the child with a mixture of affection and exasperation until she again reaches a point of impasse and the sequence recurs.

When the REFT therapist locates a sequence of significance relative to the family's problem–solution interaction, he or she then mentally arranges the actions which comprise the sequence into several steps, listing them in order of appearance. For the purposes of intervention, the sequence should be conceptualized as a circular chain involving a discrete number of steps that may be listed as occurring in a purely linear progression. The overriding conceptual basis, however, continues to be one of circular causality. The therapist, as Gurman (1981) pointed out, ". . . may choose to selectively observe a long string of interactions in this way for purposes of intervention" (p. 316). Through such selective observations, certain events become primary targets for the therapist, even though, in a circular conceptualization, they have no more determining power in the sequence than any other event. The advantage of this linear pretense is to allow the therapist greater option in deciding how to contribute to altering the sequence.

FACILITATING MORE RATIONAL FAMILY FUNCTIONING

The REFT therapist seeks to facilitate more rational functioning by assisting the troubled family system move to a place of "creative" turmoil where what was a given is augmented by new alternatives. Where alternatives are missing, there is little flexibility, and where flexibility is missing, there is no possibility of movement when faced with unhappy stagnation. The REFT therapist recognizes that the functioning of any family is constrained by two recursive complementarities: (1) between the problem at A and the efforts to solve the problem at C; and (2) between the problem at A and family members' belief at B about the problem at A. Thus, expanding either or both of these recursive complementarities through the introduction of "the meaningful new" can allow more enhancing possibilities to emerge.

The critical importance of such a stance is illuminated by Fisch et al. (1982):

But why would anyone persist in attempting solutions that do not work and, indeed, often make things progressively worse? . . . we explain the persistence of unproductive behavior on the basis of a few simple observations involving a minimum of inference and theoretical constructs: (1) From early in life, we all learn culturally standard solutions for culturally defined problems. These standard solutions often work, but sometimes they do not. Since they have been learned largely at an unconscious or an implicit level, to question or alter such solutions is very difficult. (2) When people are in stressful situations, as they are when struggling with problems, their behavior usually becomes *more* constricted and rigid. (3) Contrary to the widespread view that people are illogical, we propose that people are *too* logical; that is they act logically in terms of basic, unquestioned premises, and when undesired results occur, they employ further logical operations to explain away the discrepancy, rather than revising the premises. (p. 287)

The REFT therapist recognizes that these premises can be revised by addressing either that recursive complementarity between the presenting problem at A and the unsuccessful solution or disturbed emotional and behavioral consequences at C, or that recursive complementarity between the beliefs (B) that give meaning to the problem and the problem. Given the Rational-Emotive position's stressing the primacy of B in the therapeutic milieu, it is the latter "higher order" distinction between A and B that represents the focus for strategic change efforts—in turn contributing to breaking up the pattern of logic connecting A and C and thus eradicating the problem (and solution).

The REFT therapist begins to facilitate more rational family functioning by identifying the following sequence:

1. The interactions which the family presents as the problem to be worked on, as well as their goal relative to how the problem is to be modified.
2. The interactions which the family presents as solutions so far attempted to deal with the problem.
3. The beliefs by which the family frames how it gives meaning to the problem.

Consider, for example, a single-parent father "invested holon" who presents his daughter as having trouble adjusting to living with him. The first part of the sequence to be identified would be the father spelling out exactly what is meant by "trouble adjusting to living with him" and what he would like to see in its stead (the A). Next addressed would be a behavioral specification of those solutions that have been attempted to deal with the problem including his accompanying emotions (the C). Finally, the way in which the father discusses his daughter's problem would be assessed in order to determine how he gives meaning to/*evaluates* what is going on (the B), contributing to his apparently unsuccessful attempts to deal with the problem. This sequence would be specified à la an REFT ABC conceptualization. The father's very choice of terms in discussing the situation would be an indication of his more rational or more irrational frame of reference relative to the situation (e.g., "It's just horrible!" versus "I'm really disappointed in being stumped about this"). From this point, facilitating more rational family functioning requires moving on to an expansion of REFTs ABCs to bring strategic change processes into play.

Expanding the ABCs of REFT

After identifying ABC sequence, REFT moves on to bring strategic change processes into play. The REFT therapist begins by next seeking to contribute to changing the recursive relation between A and B. The A–B recursive relation is altered as a means of contributing to the breakup of the pattern of logic that connects the problem and attempted solutions. When that pattern is broken, the dysfunctional problem–solution relationship is disconnected with the practical consequence of eradicating the problem (and solution) and replacing them with more functional alterations.

Consider, for example, assisting parents of an acting out adolescent to alter their B from one in which they absolutistically and rigidly "demand" compliance to one wherein they conditionally and relativistically "desire" compliance. Such an alteration contributes to interrupting the kind of solution that the parents had been attempting. Within this altered A–B recursive complementarity emotional and/or behavioral overreactions to their child's misbehaviors would be less likely. Without giving up their aim of having the child comply with their requests, "desiring" would enable them to pursue solutions they would have been unable to consider in "demanding" that compliance.

Watzlawick et al. (1974) offered one such solution they called "benevolent sabotage" for managing crises between parents and rebellious teenagers. Rather than continuing to try to control their teen's behavior in a direct fashion (e.g., interrogating, scolding, punishing), the parents are instructed to announce to their adolescent that although they want him or her to comply with their requests, there is nothing they can do to guarantee control. They are then instructed to begin acting in peculiar ways in response to the teen's misbehavior. For instance, when he or she comes home late, the parents are to pretend to be asleep and to wait a long time before unlocking the door. And then, in a sincere manner, apologize for their oversight. If his clothes aren't picked up, they might "accidentally" get thrown away. As many misbehaviors of the adolescent as possible are responded to in this way. It thus becomes useless and unappealing for the adolescent to rebel, since there is little against which to rebel. By altering the parents' previous approach to solving the problem, there is no longer any interactional pattern that continues to support the problem.

This new sequence illustrates the multiple communications of stability, change, and the meaningful new characterizing of successful family therapy, that being the creation of a context wherein a family system is enabled to calibrate the way it changes in order to remain stable (Keeney & Ross, 1983). To recapitulate, the REFT therapist's facilitation of more rational family functioning began by identifying a sequence that specified the presenting problem and the intended goal (the A). Next, previously attempted solutions were assessed revealing that the parents were seeking to manage their teenager by being angrily authoritarian, punitive, and repressive (the C). The parents' B was then determined by how they presented and explained their situation. This REFT ABC analysis revealed rigid, absolutistic "demandingness" contributing to their unsuccessful and unsatisfying attempted solutions. With this information, the REFT therapist then moved to "D" (Debate), "E" (Enactment), and "F" (Feedback) in expanding the ABC analysis to bring into play strategic change processes. In so doing, the parents were helped to debate at D the effects of their "demandingness" with the potential effects of a more relativistic "desirousness" ("the meaningful new"). With this altered A–B recursive relation, they were better able to consider and then enact at E an alternative solution (i.e., "benevolent sabotage"). Then, at F, they evaluated the enactment in terms of the new solution's greater success in an affirming and a deviation-amplifying manner, fed this back to the A, which altered the A–C recursive relation. The REFT ABCDEF process is illustrated in Figure 4.1.

This REFT ABCDEF process addresses stability in terms of not deviating from the parents' original aim of having their teen behave appropriately. With respect to change, rather than continuing to demand the adolescent's compliance, they instead were facilitated in confirming

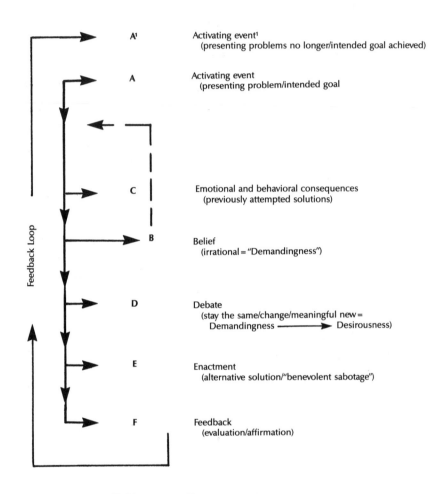

FIGURE 4.1   The REFT ABCDEF process.

the greater potential value of "desiring" that compliance which, in turn, contributed to their openness to try out a different class of solution, what appears to be a one-down position in which the parents were able to assume an overtly permissive and helpless, but covertly controlling, position in a way against which their son could not very well rebel.

In facilitating more rational family functioning, the REFT therapist continues by evaluating whether the agreed upon goals have been achieved. When the goal, usually cast in terms of problem alleviation, is achieved, efforts with the family are concluded. If a new goal is proposed, efforts can be reinitiated. If the goal is not achieved, the ABCDEF is revisited. Previous efforts are not viewed as a failure but rather as a diagnostic probe that offered further information about the family's recursive relationships between A and B, and A and C. All outcomes, whether seen as connected to the family or the therapist, are connoted in a way that provides usable feedback. Chapters 5 and 6 will now detail to a greater degree REFTs ABCDEF.

5

Family Frames of Reference

The work of Rational-Emotive Family Therapy begins by assessing family frames of reference: the cognitive, emotive, and behavioral frames family members experience relative to the concerns being offered for treatment. Assessing these frames is an ongoing process, done continually as the therapeutic process proceeds. Its purpose is to understand what is being presented so as to make suitable interventions, both at the onset of treatment and subsequently.

Assessment involves not only family members and their interactions but also the therapist and his or her interactions with them as well. The REFT therapist positions him or herself as a cybernetic therapist. As de Shazer (1985) has pointed out, not only the family members' descriptions and the therapist's descriptions of the presenting concerns, but also the therapist's interventions, family members' responses to those interventions, and the therapist's responses to the family members' responses constitute the bases of understanding family frames of reference. This process is repeated in a recursive fashion in the continuing contacts of the therapeutic system (i.e., family members and therapist).

Understanding family frames of reference requires a systemic assessment. This is much more complex than routine or perfunctory history taking. Systemic assessment incorporates the blending and interplay of both interactive and developmental data. Not only "what has happened" but "what is now happening" (here in the session) are equally important.

Inherent in assessment is a tension with intervention, between the need to gather information in order for therapeutic efforts to proceed effectively and efficiently and the desire to ameliorate presenting concerns without undue delay. Common among novice REFT therapists is the tendency to become pulled into family "crises" and then facilitate "band-aid" interventions, rather than allowing adequate time and opportunity for a full understanding of the family members' frames of reference to emerge. There are, of course, exceptions such as life-threatening situations which must be attended to before further assessment and longer-term intervention efforts can proceed. However, there is little sense in seeking to intervene if the presenting concern and goals for therapy are not clear. More often than not, such "band-aid" interventions normally reflect the "more of the same" misguided solution that has brought the family to therapy in the first place.

Before describing the procedures involved in assessing family frames of references within REFT, it is prudent to offer several prefacing remarks in order to place the assessement process into proper perspective. One such remark concerns the questions of "when" and "how much time" is required. In REFT, the assessment process begins with the first contact with a family, and, depending upon the therapist's expertise and the complexity of the family's presenting concerns, it can take only a portion of the first session or several sessions. Experienced REFT therapists can usually facilitate an adequate assessment and begin introducing strategic change processes by the end of the first session or early in the second session. It is a mistake to think that assessment requires a long time to assemble and that it must be perfectly in place before strategic change processes can be introduced.

As a second prefacing remark, it is important to consider that the overall therapy situation will best dictate when and how assessment will occur. The procedures described in this chapter pertain to a "standard" therapy setting where a family has sought the therapist's assistance and presents as motivated to some degree to work toward problem resolution. Many times the benefits of a motivated family and a clearly defined therapy setting are not enjoyed (e.g., "invested holon" parents seeking assistance relative to their adult child's drug abuse; the adult child denying any problem); assessment as well as facilitating strategic change processes may by necessity be delivered in something other than textbook fashion. However, the basic procedures presented in this chapter form a solid foundation which can be adapted and delivered in innovative ways in difficult circumstances.

Finally, it is helpful to recognize the major goal for assessing family frames of reference as being "Rational-Emotive Insight" (Greiger & Boyd, 1980): the therapeutic system (i.e., the therapist and family members together) gaining understanding of and being able to openly acknowledge the primary contributors to the presenting problems.

Rational-Emotive insight can be best viewed as being a certain minimal "need to know" construct. This construct incorporates three major determinations: (1) the problem; (2) the manner in which the problem is evaluated; and (3) the solutions being attempted to deal with the problem. These three determinations constitute the A, the B, and the C of REFT respectively. Following, the general rule of thumb for assessing family frames of reference is: Start with A, tie A to C, get B. The order is not invariable, however, it is the most common order for assessing the ABCs of REFT.

IDENTIFYING AND CLARIFYING THE A

Identifying the A begins by asking, "What are the concerns that bring you all here today?" Related questions focus on why treatment was sought now and how the present therapist was chosen. These questions are best phrased with an eye to obtaining descriptions of interactional sequences that resemble the script of a screen play. For example, if a parent says, "That kid is just no good," the therapist might ask, "In what ways is he no good and how do you react to him when he acts in these ways?"

In many cases, the family members offer the answers the therapist is seeking, for example:

FATHER: Our son ignores our requests that he keep his room clean and we've just about given up.
MOTHER: Dad's right. All we seem to do is remind, remind, and remind him to clean up his room.

In other cases, however, family members' responses need clarification, for instance, "We aren't communicating." When the report is too vague to provide a screen play picture of the presenting concern, more focused questioning is called for. Further, the therapist will request information about how the presenting concern is interfering with family life; what it prevents family members from doing or makes them do unwillingly (Segal & Kahn, 1986).

As family members relate their concerns, the therapist seeks to be attuned to two major elements: (1) how the family members *describe, and/or infer* what has been happening, and (2) how the family members *evaluate* what has been happening. The first element is the A, the Activating Event; the latter relates to the B, their rational and/or irrational beliefs about A. The A entails family members *descriptions and inferences* whereas the B is their *evaluation* relative to their descriptions and inferences. For example, a child shares her extreme upset about her father, "He's so unfair because he won't let me stay out after 10 P.M. with the kids at Ann's house next door." The A here is the father's unfairness in not allowing his daughter to stay out past 10 P.M. It is an inference (a description would be a simply stated fact, e.g., "My father has told me I must be in by 10 P.M."). Whether her father may or may not be unfair is in and of itself (even if most any objective observer would judge him to truly be very unfair), insufficient to trigger the girl's extreme upset. For her to become extremely upset, she would need to evaluate her inference that her father was unfair in a certain manner. For example, were she to state further that his unfairness was utterly *horrible* or that he *must not* be unfair, these addenda would constitute *evaluations*. This distinction between inference and evaluation in particular is a crucial one for the REFT therapist. In the example above, the daughter could conclude that her father unfairly enforces her 10 P.M. curfew, yet not upset herself about that inference. How? By not *evaluating* this inference (A) as something so "horrible" and not "demanding" that he be fair. Thus, if at B, she maintained a view that although her father was acting unfairly, he was still trying to do his best for her, she would likely, at C, feel and act quite differently about the situation. This, in turn, would tend to feed back to A being perceived as less severe of a "problem."

To facilitate identification of the A, it is preferable to tie the presenting concerns to goals for therapy. Following the initial inquiry "What are the concerns that bring you here today?" with a statement such as "In answering that question, you might want to focus on how you would like things to be different" sets a goal-oriented tone. Ideally, this goal-setting process would follow a three-step process either explicitly outlined or implicitly engaged in with family members interacting among themselves, the therapist offering only those prompts necessary to maintain the goal orientation while observing the transactions that occur. This predominantly family-member interaction tends to offer valuable assessment information. Frequently families will "live out" their presenting problem in the session itself as they become actively involved with each other, as opposed to only listening. The information gained from this interaction will be particularly helpful in assessing not only the A, but even more so, the B and C. The three steps in the process include:

1. Brainstorm all possible concerns (i.e., "Let's try to come up with all the ways you'd like to see each other acting, feeling, thinking differently. . . . how you'd like things to be. We're just seeking possible ideas now without a commitment to any just yet. . . .").
2. Prioritize the 2, 3, or 4 major concerns (i.e., "Given you've identified all these potential goals. . . . which of them would be your #1 priority. . . .your #2 priority. . . . your #3 priority. . . ?").
3. Further concretize each prioritized concern by establishing "benchmarks" indicating how movement toward goal attainment might be recognized (i.e., "Relative to your #1 priority . . . what might be an event or circumstance, that when occurring, you'd be able to say to yourselves and/or each other, 'We're making progress toward our goal?' ").

This framing defines the presenting concerns to be addressed, as well as specifies the goals of therapy in terms of how these concerns are to be modified and subsequent circumstances envisioned.

MAKING THE A–C CONNECTION

Since REFT sees problems as persisting because of the unsuccessful efforts of family members to solve them, the therapist must next obtain an understanding of how said problems have been behaviorally dealt with and the emotional accompaniment to those dealings. This is the C of the ABCs of REFT, the behavioral and emotional *consequences*. Remembering the rule of thumb posited earlier, "Start with A, tie A to C, get B," emphasis is now placed on what is currently being done to solve the problems (achieve the goals) delineated in identifying and clarifying the A. The questions to guide this part of the assessment process: "What have you been trying to do to deal with the problems (reach the prioritized goals) you identified?" and relative to each response therein "How do you feel when attempting to do so in the way you just described?" The latter question aims at identifying an emotional state while the former aims at a screenplay description of a behavioral solution sequence.

In assessing behavioral and emotional consequences, it is important to do so within the context of the identified As. Thus, it is valuable to return to the prioritized treatment goals and their accompanying benchmarks and ascertain the symptomatic behavioral solution sequences and emotions that accompany the family members' expressed concerns and desires. This is referred to as the *A–C Connection*. Normally each treatment goal in order of its priority and its identified benchmarks are addressed individually in determining the relative A–C connections. The first prioritized goal is then assessed relative to its accompanying B, to be followed by strategic intervention for that goal at REFTs D, E, and F. Assuming intervention has been successful, the A–C connection is then assessed for the second prioritized treatment goal, its accompanying B, followed by D, E, and F and so on until each goal has been adequately addressed. Often, the same or similar A–C connections, Bs, and intervention strategies are relative to many or all of the treatment goals and thus assessment and intervention relative to the first prioritized goal generalizes to the others, making further efforts less necessary.

Persons vary widely in the extent to which they can accurately describe their behavioral solution sequences and accompanying feelings. Some articulate family members, particularly parents, older children, or those having had previous therapy experiences, can be surprising helpful. Others, particularly younger children, express "I don't know," or only very vague responses needing to be further expounded upon and clarified. For these latter family members especially, it is critical to utilize the A as a cue. In hearing family members relay their expressed concerns, goals relating to these concerns, and benchmarks indicating how they will know when these goals are being attained, the therapist must listen to how they felt and acted in the experiencing of that activating event. While listening, *observation* is also a tipoff to their emotions and behavioral solution sequences as they will frequently act them out in interaction with each other and the therapist in the session itself.

Congruence between emotions and behavioral solution sequences are another guide for the therapist to consider. Because emotions and behavioral solution sequences are contingently linked together, knowing one will often illuminate the other. When two parents express how they yell at their children as a means of stopping the complaints about each other, it can be inferred that they were likely angry. If they say that they felt hopeless and like giving up, the therapist might expect avoidant, nonassertive behavioral solution sequences under most conditions. If, in session, the parents denied having anger toward their children, yet made disparaging remarks to them, the therapist could be fairly confident that they were nonetheless angry. In such instances behavioral solution sequences provide a clue to emotion, and vice versa.

Finally, it is helpful for the therapist to remember that there are only a limited number of major emotions as well as behavioral solution sequences that most families experience at specific transition points in their family life cycle. Therefore, it is best to look for the simple and expected as opposed to the more uncommon and esoteric. The search is for as concrete as possible a framing that describes the attempted behavioral solution sequences and accompanying emotions for each presenting concern as expressed by the prioritized treatment goals and identified benchmarks; a C connection for each A.

Moving to the B

Although family members may try a variety of problem-solving attempts, there is usually a common denominator or "family rule" that appears to guide these problem solving efforts (Segal & Kahn, 1986). For example, two "invested holon" parents' presenting complaint was their teenage daughter's noncompliance. Their prioritized goal was to have her obey them more readily; following which they identified several specific "house rules," which if attended to more closely by the daughter, would offer benchmarks relative to their goal's being attained. In assessing their A–C connection, the parents listed a number of solutions they had been unsuccessfully attempting. "We've done just about everything imaginable. "We've warned her, taken away her allowance and other money privileges. We've grounded her for weeks at a time. We've sat her down and explained that this is our house and she has to abide by our rules. Several times, we even hit her. We've tried to keep her away from those lowlife friends of hers who are constantly in trouble by sending her to a private school. She was expelled after a month and a half. We've tried just about everything we can." "Everything," however, consisted of variations of the same belief accompanying all these attempted solutions: "She *must* obey us."

It is this belief, framing how family members evaluate the A, and following, contributes to the C, that represents the final major assessment determinant. While it is not always possible to subsume the primary problem (prioritized goal) family members have presented under one basic belief (B), usually most, and certainly those most pernicious problems tend to fall into one major category of irrationality. Apparent exceptions are likely to be of secondary importance and are best deferred for later consideration if necessary.

In REFT, the term *belief* is the central explanatory construct, and it is thus critical that therapists accurately understand the meaning of this term in order to assess it. Eschenroeder's (1982) description of the B is a valuable one in this regard:

> The B-element of the ABC refers to rather different phenomena: (1) *thoughts* and *images*, which can be observed through introspection by the individual; (2) *unconscious processes*, which can be inferred post hoc from the individual's feelings and behavior ("unconscious verbalizations"); (3) the *belief system* underlying the person's thoughts, emotions, and behaviors. (p. 275)

Thus, belief can be viewed as a construct that embraces at least three distinct subclasses of cognitive phenomena: (1) thoughts that family members are thinking and are aware of at a given time about A; (2) thoughts about A that family members are not immediately aware of; and (3) more abstract thoughts that family members may hold in general (Bernard, 1981).

Beliefs are not always easy for family members to verbalize since much of the human thinking process consists of greatly overlearned cognitive habits which have become automatic. The more abstract beliefs, in particular, that family members maintain are typically unspoken overtly, as well as covertly in self-talk. These abstract beliefs, however, can be considered relatively enduring evaluations that affect family members' descriptions and inferences at A, and in doing so, contribute to subsequent behavioral solution sequences and emotional responses at C. They are frequently an expression of the values of family members and as such play an important role in explaining to the therapist and family members alike basic goals and purposes. Family values extend to things such as love, approval, achievement and the like. It is the degree, however, to which these values are prized which influences the actions and emotions of family members. Extreme valuations of, for example, family togetherness would likely (but not always) contribute to seeking to enforce rigid family boundaries in members' interactions with those outside the family, accompanying needless unhappiness, and therefore may constitute "irrationality."

In terms of the ABC model, it is important for therapists to continually stress for themselves in assessing family members' beliefs that rational beliefs generally contribute to more constructive behavioral solution sequences and more moderate emotions. Rational beliefs may contribute to intense levels of some emotions that are at times appropriate, such as intense sadness upon the death of a loved one. Irrational beliefs contribute to maintaining unsuccessful behavioral solution sequences and extremely stressful emotions, all of which make it quite difficult to address more adaptively their problem situation.

As discussed in Chapter 2, irrational beliefs which family members hold and that frequently contribute to unsuccessful behavioral solution sequences and extremely stressful emotions tend to derive from a basic irrational *demandingness* or "must" (Ellis, 1980):

1. I *must* do well and win approval for my performances, or else I rate as a rotten person.
2. Others *must* treat me considerately and kindly in precisely the way I want them to treat me; if they don't society and the universe should severly blame, damn, and punish them for their inconsiderateness.
3. Conditions under which I live *must* get arranged so that I get practically everything I want comfortably, quickly, and easily, and get virtually nothing that I don't want. (pp. 5–7)

The Rational-Emotive position further stresses that there are three primary forms of thinking that emanate from this basic irrational demandingness ("must") (Ellis, 1980):

1. *Devastation Beliefs/Awfulizing* ("It is awful, or terrible, or horrible that we are not doing as we must").
2. *Discomfort Disturbance Beliefs/We Can't Stand-it-itis* ("We can't stand, can't bear the things that are happening to us that must not happen!").
3. *Denigration Beliefs/Worthlessness* ("We are worthless persons if we don't do as well and win as much approval as we must").

Family members' thoughts or self-talk that they are able to observe through introspection will normally be volunteered easily. The following questions posed to family members often facilitate their observations of major irrational beliefs (Ellis, 1977):

1. Look for your demandingness. Ask yourselves: "What should or *must* we keep saying about our situation?"
2. Look for your awfulizing. Ask yourselves: "What do we think is awful about our situation?"
3. Look for something you think you all can't stand. Ask yourselves: "What is it about our situation we think we can't bear?"
4. Look for your damning of yourselves or others. Ask yourselves: "In what manner are we damning or downing anyone in connection with what's going on in our situation?"

More frequently and intensely impacting on family members' circumstances, however, are their unconscious verbalizations and more general abstract beliefs. Most family members have probably never been asked to investigate these latter beliefs, let alone report their thoughts to someone else. Many family members, particularly children, may not have a sufficient vocabulary to describe the thoughts they experience. Other family members, when asked what they might have been thinking, respond with feelings (e.g., "I'm sad, angry, depressed, etc."). The therapist's task is one of facilitating family members identifying and communicating their thoughts (i.e., evaluations of A).

Walen, et al. (1980) offered several questions to elicit cognitive responses:

1. What were you thinking? (or, if in a session, "What are you thinking right now?")
2. What might have been a sentence you were telling yourself?
3. Were you aware of any thoughts in your head?
4. There goes that old record again; what was it playing this time?

If family members claim no thoughts were present, the therapist may need to spend time modeling how to tune into and monitor their thinking. By synthesizing information offered by family members about their activating events, behavioral solution sequences, and accompanying emotions, therapists can infer the presence of specific beliefs which they can then model. For example:

"I don't know exactly what your specific thought might be, but many kids when feeling upset and faced with a situation such as you describe often are thinking something like this to themselves. . . ."

or

"In my experience when couples have a great deal of difficulty accommodating each other, they're often saying to themselves something on the order of. . . ."

It will be important, of course, to validate these suggestions by seeking family members' confirmation; for instance, "How might something like that fit with your situation?" or "Does that sound familiar?"

Frequently, family members will talk to themselves in what, syntactically, are half-sentences. In essence, they have punctuated their verbalization with a period, although the thought is not consciously completed (Walen et al., 1980). Consider the following illustration:

ADOLESCENT: For a long time I didn't think about anybody but me.
THERAPIST: And now that I'm thinking more about the family. . . ?
ADOLESCENT: I've decided that I want to help out more, but I just can't get started doing so.

In this illustration, the therapist feeds the thought back to the adolescent as a sentence-completion task.

Recalling that it is the evaluation that represents the B of REFT, family members may verbalize only one part of their thinking, leaving the evaluative portion unstated. The therapist will need to append the unstated evaluation, most appropriately offered as a hypothesis. For example:

TEENAGER #1: Mom and Dad are just being totally unfair. . . .
TEENAGER #2: Yeah. They never give us a break at all. . . .
THERAPIST: And they *must* not be unfair or give you a break for any reason?

Missing thoughts can also form the ending of a syllogism. Consider the following statement from two parents presenting with debilitating depression: "If she truly loved us, she'd show us the respect we deserve as her parents." These parents may stop their verbalization at this point; the question of concern to the therapist would be why then are these people so depressed. The therapist's query at this point might entail asking them what they conclude about these circumstances. Most likely, they have finished their syllogism covertly: "Therefore she doesn't love us and that's utterly *awful.*" Moving later to REFT's D, E, and F, reflection on the logic of this structure will reveal that "if–then" statements do not necessarily follow this one pattern; for example, there could be many other reasons for their daughter's demeanor, and even if she does not respect them, is this so *utterly* bad?

A related practice used to arrive at more specific irrational beliefs relative to the A being presented is to lead family members through a chain of thoughts by repeating a simple question. Consider the couple who report their inability to pursue a singular solution:

THERAPIST: How is it you are stuck in pursuing this one solution with the kids when it's not working as well as you'd like?
HUSBAND: Well, it works some of the time.
THERAPIST: But how is it you stick with this one solution especially when it only works some of the time, and not enough to satisfy you?
WIFE: But if we tried something else and it didn't work, we'd feel pretty stupid.

THERAPIST: Well, that's how you might feel, but what would that mean for the
            two of you?
HUSBAND: It would prove that her parents (meaning his wife's) are right when
            they say we're inadequate as parents.
WIFE: He's right.

Similarly, a chain of time-projection questions may be enlightening:

THERAPIST: Let's just suppose that you're not able to adopt the child you've
            met right away; not that you won't, but let's just suppose for a mo-
            ment that you won't.
HUSBAND: We'd never get over it.
(Wife nods in agreement)
THERAPIST: How is it that you'd *never* get over it.
HUSBAND: We'd never find anyone else.
THERAPIST: That is a possibility, although very unlikely. But what if you didn't
            find a child to adopt? What would that be like for you?
WIFE: That would be utterly horrible; having to live our life out alone.

As the example illustrates, this couple's irrational belief is one of devastation and hopelessness resulting in present and potential solutions of
maintaining their current unsatisfactory upsettedness and sense of dire
urgency or having no other alternative but being childless. This irrational belief blocks pursuit of potential alternative solutions.

Bernard and Joyce (1984) compiled a number of assessment methods
which can be utilized to facilitate eliciting family members' thoughts;
to enable them to describe their evaluations orally in a manner which
will further their understanding as well as contribute to moving to the B.

Thought bubbles can be utilized to convey the general idea that thoughts
contribute to unsuccessful behavioral solution sequences and accompanying upsetting emotions, as well as assisting family members to verbalize their beliefs. For example, in a series of cartoons, it is possible
to illustrate different temporally related scenes that illustrate the presenting problem of the family. Empty bubbles appear over the characters
in each scene. The emotional expressions on the faces of the characters
help to dramatize the scenes, and family members are asked to fill in
the bubble above his or her corresponding character with what he or
she thinks that character is thinking.

The sentence completion technique can be employed to elicit family
members' beliefs. The therapist develops several incomplete sentences
that tap relevant introspective information. Examples include:

(a) When the kids don't do what we ask of them, we think. . . .
(b) We're most unhappy at home when we're thinking. . . .
(c) Mom and Dad's high expectations contribute to our thinking. . . .

Think-aloud approaches (Genest & Turk, 1981) involve the therapist assigning family members a task and requesting them to think out loud as they are undertaking it. For example, two parents and their teenage daughter having problems agreeing on a weekend curfew for the daughter might be asked to spend 10 minutes attempting to come to some agreement. Before attempting to speak to each other, each family member would "think aloud his or her thoughts about what he or she is about to say.

"And," "but," and *"because"* (Hauck, 1980) are extremely useful words that the therapist can use to assist family members to tune into and verbalize their beliefs. If a family member pauses at the end of what seems to be an incomplete sentence about what he or she is thinking (i.e., without reporting an evaluation), the therapist can coax the family member along with words such as "and," "but," and "because."

Instant replay (Bedford, 1974) is a technique wherein the therapist requests that family members keep track of situations and events between sessions that result in unpleasant emotions ("rough spots"). During the next session, family members are asked to do a "rerun" or "instant replay" of the rough spot conveying the thoughts they remember having or probably had in relation to the rough spot.

Guided imagery (Meichenbaum, 1977) involves the therapist asking family members to relax and then to imagine as vividly as possible a problem situation and to focus on what they are thinking. Family members are requested to describe the scene and then are further encouraged to communicate their thoughts associated with the setting.

The TAT-like approach (Meichenbaum, 1977) is an elicitational method that can be helpful when more direct techniques are not successful. This method uses pictures of ambiguous family situations selected for their relevance to the family's activating events. Family members are asked to make up a story, primarily focusing on the thoughts of the characters as well as what they might do about the situation and any accompanying feelings.

A CAVEAT: DICHOTOMOUS THINKING AND THE B

Many family members tend to categorize their thoughts dichotomously; that is, in "black or white," "either-or" terms. They believe the only way

Demandingness	Desirousness	Don't Care
irrational	rational	irrational

FIGURE 5.1   The irrational—rational—irrational continuum of Demandingness —Desirousness—Don't Care.

they can think is the way they are presently (e.g., demanding, or awful-izing), or totally the opposite (e.g., not caring, or as if nothing has hap-pened). They frequently recognize the poor problem-solving position their irrational beliefs contribute to but are understandably stuck there when not caring, denial, and the like are perceived as their only other alternatives. This is often an issue of critical importance when first at-tempting to move on to the B; an issue contributing to a reluctance to consider further the impact of B, or at times, premature termination.

Beliefs occur on a continuum; there is the "mid-range" in which ra-tional beliefs tend to lie; the extremes representing more irrational beliefs.

Demandingness/Desirousness/Don't Care

Demandingness is believing that certain things must or must not hap-pen. Horney (1942) aptly coined the phrase "the tyranny of the should" to describe this type of dysfunctional thinking. Often, family members' first reaction to the idea that their demands are hurting them is that one is proposing they adopt an "I don't care" attitude. Ellis (1962) stressed that the major feature of rational beliefs is that they reflect personal pref-erences, wants, or desires. Rational beliefs become irrational when family members convert these preferences, wants, or desires into absolutistic musts, have to's, and demands or conversely into an "I don't care" de-meanor (*Authors' note:* actually "I *must* not care"). REFT posits that a *desir-ing* evaluation is more adaptive and productive than a *demanding* or an *I don't care* evaluation. This continuum is illustrated in Figure 5.1 above.

Devastation/Disappointment/Denial

Devastation is the belief that certain things are awful, horrible, terrible, catastrophic, devastating. Consider the meaning of being "devastated." Devastating, of course, means bad. But even more than that, it means for most persons the worst thing that could happen—100% bad (Wessler & Wessler, 1980). Philosophically, nothing is 100% bad because some-

Devastation	Disappointment	Denial
irrational	rational	irrational

FIGURE 5.2   The irrational—rational—irrational continuum of Devastation—Disappointment—Denial.

thing worse could always happen. For example, some family members would consider a divorce the worst thing that could happen to them. This might be 99% bad, but 99.1% bad might be divorce occurring simultaneously with a major illness in the family. Thus, the relative badness of an event can be judged by determining what could be worse. The reaction of many family members to the idea that "nothing is devastating" is that it is being suggested that nothing should be judged as bad—*denial*. Badness obviously does exist. However, it is a matter of degree. Neither minimizing nor maximizing problems are generally helpful in contributing to more successful Cs. Rather, REFT proposes that the rational alternative to devastation and denial is a more midrange degree of badness (assuming that most persons would see the A as a negative event) or *disappointment*. This continuum is illustrated in Figure 5.2 above.

Discomfort Disturbance/Discomfort Tolerance/Discomfort Denial

Most people want their family life to flow as easily as possible. They seek to enjoy themselves, avoid pain and difficulty, get what they want without too much effort, hassle, or delay, and experience unhappiness infrequently and then only in mild degrees. Many, when frustrated, react with displeasure, moan and groan for awhile, and then quickly get on with their daily business. Ellis (1977) has proposed, however, that a good proportion of the population tends to frequently go beyond just wanting things to go well and view it as utterly tragic when things do not. *Discomfort disturbance* stems from family members' recognition that their comfort is threatened and that (1) they *should* or *must* get what they want (and *should not* or *must not* get what they don't want) and (2) it is *awful* or *catastrophic* when they don't get what they must. Rather than merely disliking hurt or pain, and desiring comfort, these family members fear or dread discomfort and experience self-pity, impatience, and low frustration. As with the demandingness/desirousness/don't care continuum, frequently family members' initial response to the idea that their extreme and intense dislike of discomfort is hurting them is

Discomfort Disturbance	Discomfort Tolerance	Discomfort Denial
irrational	rational	irrational

FIGURE 5.3   The irrational—rational—irrational continuum of Discomfort Disturbance—Discomfort Tolerance—Discomfort Denial.

that they take on an ambivalent, I don't care attitude. The absolutistic need to be comfortable usually prevents family members from considering, let alone attempting, alternative solution sequences. The ability to tolerate discomfort and frustration, not for its own sake, but so that constructive change can occur, is a rational belief. It is a critical contributor to the potential acquisition of a philosophy of long-range hedonism—the pursuit of meaningful long-term goals while tolerating the deprivation of attractive short-term goals which are self-defeating in the longer term. This continuum is illustrated in Figure 5.3 above.

Denigration/Acceptance/Deification

Denigration implies that "We ourselves (or others) are *horrible* for doing something that we (or they) *must* not do." Denigration involves two evaluative processes (Dryden, 1984): (1) the process of rating our own self-hood (or the person-hood of others) as totally bad, and (2) "devil-ifying ourselves (or others) for being totally bad. This latter process emanates from a commonly accepted theological theme that as a "devil," one rots in hell forever. If this devil-ifying process did not occur, family members could theoretically regard themselves (or others) as totally bad at present but with the future potential for good. In suggesting, however, that theirs' or others' "self" is not good, the "is" of identity is being employed which means: self = badness, and this is a fundamental core of what we or others shall always be. The opposite end of this continuum represents the equally irrational rating of their own or others' selves as good *(deification)*. Earlier in his formulations, Ellis advocated that persons consider themselves and others to be "good" because they were alive. Some, however, asserted that they could just as well be "bad" because they were alive. Ellis then suggested that persons rate their "aliveness" and "striving for personal fulfillment" as good and proposed that self-and-other rating impeded this process and was thus irrational. He noticed, however, that most persons tended to rate themselves globally (either positive or negative) after doing or not doing something. Thereafter, he posited self or other rating as a conditional process: one

Denigration	Acceptance	Deification
irrational	rational	irrational

FIGURE 5.4 The irrational—rational—irrational continuum of Denigration— Acceptance—Deification.

was good if certain conditions applied, or bad (or less good) if other conditions applied. Ellis' solution was to identify an unconditional process: *acceptance.* Acceptance is the rational alternative to denigrating or deifying ratings. It might be expressed in family members' belief "We can accept ourselves or others as fallibly human no matter what." This continuum is illustrated in Figure 5.4.

RATIONAL-EMOTIVE INSIGHT REVISITED

This chapter began by stressing the primary goal for assessing family frames of reference as Rational-Emotive insight wherein the therapeutic system (i.e., therapist and family members) gains understanding of, and is consequently able to openly acknowledge, the primary contributors to the concerns being presented for therapy. Grieger and Boyd (1980) asserted that this insight tends to have at least four significant benefits:

Issues Are Clarified. By the time they seek therapy, most family members are very frustrated and a good number are actually quite despondent and at their wits' end. They have ruminated and worried for countless hours about their concerns; they have consulted with friends, read books, attended lectures, and have attempted what they perceived as all sorts of solutions, all to little or no avail. Their primary problem is that they have, at best, only a vague notion of what the problematic issues are. Therefore, their various efforts at finding relief have been fruitless. Rational-emotive insight serves to clarify for family members the primary loci of their problems and offers a structure for beginning to take a new direction. Thus, they gain a better understanding of the issues and a foundation for change efforts.

Hope Is Promoted/Motivation Is Facilitated. A major concern for many family members are their profound feelings of helplessness, hopelessness, and utter frustration. They tend to believe that there is nothing they can do to bring about significant change in their circumstances. This contributes discouragement and a paucity of motivation to actively work for change. Rational-Emotive insight tends to promote a sense of hope and power as well as an eagerness to participate in therapy. Formulating goals at A, recognizing the connection of C to A, and then being illuminated by the impact of B are all certainly therapeutic gains in and of themselves, but they also contribute to increased hope and motivation in gaining the structure this process provides.

Rapport Is Built. Facilitation of Rational-Emotive insight tends to establish therapist credibility and promote excellent rapport between the therapist and family members. Family members frequently report they have never been listened to so well and never been understood with such depth, at least not so quickly as by their REFT therapist. Perhaps this is due to the REFT therapist interacting with the family relative to the basic values and philosophies contributing to their feelings and actions, rather than the more superficial material to which many other therapists of different persuasions attend. Clearly, family members' sense of being immediately and profoundly understood by and involved with the therapist enhances their receptivity to REFT.

REFT Makes Greater Sense. REFT is not what many family members bargain for when they first enter therapy. Some expect the therapist to be a supportive paternal or maternal figure who sits back, listens, and lets them pour out their troubles. Others think of their prospective therapist in the same mold as the family physician who briefly listens to complaints, provokes and probes for a few moments, and then writes a prescription that quickly alleviates symptoms. In contrast, the REFT therapist is an active, directive, challenging system member. The REFT therapist as cybernetic therapist requests substantial efforts from both him or herself and family members in the therapy efforts. If family members' expectations conflict with what the therapist presents, there is a danger that they will be turned off or scared off by what they encounter. Rational–Emotive insight early in the therapy process is a precaution against early termination, for this insight contributes to REFT and the experience of family therapy being understandable and acceptable.

6

Strategic Change Processes

Having assessed the family's frames of reference, REFT strategic change begins by being quite clear about what to *stay away from*. Fisch et al. (1982) refer to this as the "mine field." Much intersession or presession planning should center around the therapist asking him or herself, "What do I most want us to avoid?" This answer is primarily indicated by the main thrust of the family's beliefs relative to the activating events identified. Thus, for example, to the parents who habitually demanded compliance from their teenage daughter, agreeing that they should be stronger in their demands to gain compliance would be avoided. By recognizing what to avoid, at least little if anything, would be added to the maintenance of the family's problem. More importantly, however, knowing what to avoid provides, by contrast, basic direction toward formulating the strategic thrust indicated in a case.

Knowing what to avoid will help keep the therapeutic system (therapist and family members) out of hot water, but movement can come only from actions guided by a strategy of treatment. Effective strategies are likely to be those in the opposite direction of the family's basic thrust (Fisch et al., 1982). They are also those strategies that incorporate the multiple communications of stability, change, and the meaningful new characterizing successful family therapy; that being the creation of a context wherein a family system is enabled to calibrate the way it changes in order to remain stable (Keeney & Ross, 1983). In REFT, this means moving from irrational beliefs to more rational beliefs at D (Debate); then on to E (Enactment) where new alternative solutions are attempted; followed by F (Feedback) where the new solutions are evaluated and this information fed back to A.

A number of specific methods commonly used by REFT therapists will be presented in this chapter. These methods will not form an exhaustive list. The major point to recall throughout, however, is that the REFT therapist can best be seen as a teacher and family members as students in a common new learning experience. The effective teacher is one who provides a variety of learning experiences and who does not just lecture, but actively involves the students in the learning process through an assortment of outside assignments and in-class discussions and simulations. REFT therapists similarly use an assortment of outside assignments (homework) and in-session discussions and simulations. Further, and like the effective teacher, the REFT therapist respects family members in accepting no nonsense and actively confronting them with the deleterious contributions their irrational beliefs make to their lives. In doing so, however, the REFT therapist seeks to communicate a strong sense of encouragement at all times (i.e., "I know you can do it") (Wessler & Wessler, 1980). Finally, the REFT therapist seeks to actively learn about him or herself all the while as well.

Let us now move more directly to these strategic change processes, the D, E, and F of REFT.

DEBATE: GENERAL STRATEGIES

What is a debate? Webster's (1976) defines it as "a process wherein a question is discussed by considering opposing arguments." In REFT debate (D) is a challenge to family members to consider the opposing arguments being presented by their irrational and rational beliefs. Once family members' basic irrational beliefs have been assessed, the essence of D is to pursue three main tasks: The first task is to facilitate considerable cognitive dissonance for family members by coupling their basic irrational belief with its rational counterpart and then compiling disconfirming evidence relative to their irrational belief; the second task is family members' exploration of the more rational counterpart to their irrational belief in a way that affirms the greater helpfulness and sensibility of the rational belief; and the third task is to review and confirm how the irrational belief contributes to their distressful emotions and unsuccessful behavioral solution sequences while the more rational belief would likely offer enhanced opportunity for greater emotional satisfaction (or less dissatisfaction) and successful behavioral solution sequences.

Family members are offered the irrational and rational options available to them, and are asked to examine each, bit by bit, to see which makes better sense and is more helpful. Debate is then a logical and empirical process in which family members are facilitated in stopping and critically thinking. Its basic goal is for family members to select the most adaptive philosophy available to them. In REFT, this more adaptive philosophy is characterized by rational beliefs such as: "It would be sad if we can't get what we want right now, but we'll be able to stand it," or "We weren't able to succeed here, but we are fallible, and that's certainly not devastating." This basic goal in REFT thus represents *second order change*; that being a change in the rules that govern the family system.

Debate begins with the therapist introducing cognitive dissonance with regard to family members' basic irrational belief by presenting the rational counterpart to that irrational belief relative to their prioritized A in a manner that says to them *"Stay the same."* For example, to the family with a B of "We must never argue!" the therapist would communicate, "When disagreements arise, your *desire* not to argue is an important one." Debate proceeds with the therapist then communicating *"But change."* To continue with the above example: ". . . . your desire not to argue is an important one. However, the belief that you *must absolutely never* argue as opposed to merely desiring not to argue appears to be hurting you as disagreements remain unsettled or are settled unsatisfactorily. *"The meaningful new"* is provided as the therapist then stresses the importance of the family members *debating* the past and/or potential hurtfulness or helpfulness of each, the irrational belief and the rational belief, in contributing to more satisfying emotions and successful behavioral solution sequences. Debate concludes with a confirmation of the benefits of adopting the more rational belief.

The major form of debate in REFT is cognitive. Cognitive debate relies primarily on the verbal interchange between therapist and family members, among family members themselves, as well as within the minds of all these individuals. In employing cognitive debate as a strategic change process, it is important to recognize that while the irrational belief may initially appear to be the focal point, its rational counterpart represents the consequent deduction which should similarly and equally be challenged. Debate relative to the irrational belief will be stressed here as once that hurdle is cleared, the hurdles of challenging the rational counterpart and confirming its greater potential will follow summarily. Walen et al. (1980) described four predominant forms of cognitive debate: questioning, didactic, exaggeration, and vicarious modeling.

Questioning as a debate strategy can be employed in three ways. The first of these ways asks for evidence, logical consistency, or semantic clarity in family members' thinking. For example:

82364

T: Ken's life may be much tougher if he doesn't finish school. Where's the evidence that he's therefore a total failure?

or

T: No one wants Ken to make a mistake. But where does it follow that he must absolutely not make a mistake?

or

T: Of course, you are all disappointed by Ken's not finishing school. Do you have to be destroyed, though?

The second form of questioning requests that family members reevaluate whether future events will occur and if so, whether they will be unpleasant as they believe. These questions are particularly useful in debating devastation and discomfort beliefs. For example:

T: Mom and Dad's divorce will surely create difficulties that all of you will likely find uncomfortable adjusting to. Assuming that all families experiencing divorce go through this, what do you expect to be so terrible that none of you will be able to stand it?

or

T: Mom and Dad are divorcing and you probably won't see each of them as often and that is disappointing to think about. Can you explain how that's the worst thing that could ever happen to you?

The third form of questioning does not challenge the logic of family members' thinking as much as it serves to help them assess the hedonistic value of their beliefs. To illustrate:

T: It is important to be cautious in thinking about how Jennifer might take on greater self-responsibility. As long as you believe that you must be overly-protective though, how is she going to mature?

or

T: I can appreciate your desire to shelter Jennifer from the harder tasks of life. Is it worth the risk to keep her a "psychological" child for too long a period, just because you think something horrible might confront her?

In using questioning as a debate strategy, therapists want to be sure to allow family members time to consider and fully contemplate the questions asked. Only one question at a time should be asked and answers to the questions should not be given, at least until family members have been afforded an opportunity to search for their own answers. Silences should be expected.

Primarily because many of these questions have no logical answer, family members are likely to feel discomfort, sometimes significant discomfort depending upon their beliefs about answering. For instance:

T: Where is the evidence that the children *must* do that?
FM: (long silence) I guess there really isn't any.

It is important that the therapist, while awaiting a response, seek to observe any nonverbal signs of discomfort which family members may be exhibiting. If any are appearing exceptionally distressed, it may be helpful to do a brief ABC. Perhaps irrational devastation beliefs about not knowing the "right" answers are contributing to anxious feelings and a behavioral solution sequence of silence. Attending to this irrational belief will tend to allow the original debate to continue more fruitfully.

Another point for the therapist to attend to in employing a questioning debate strategy is a frequent response of many family members, that of giving a rational belief as an answer to a critical question about an irrational belief. Consider for example, the therapist requesting family members to debate their devastation belief about Father not getting his job promotion. Their first response is a justification of why the situation is *disappointing:*

T: I recognize that it would be discouraging if, Dad, you don't get that promotion you're up for. How is it however that you all would have to see it as so utterly *awful?*
FM: Because we'd all feel bad for him.

Here the family member is failing to discriminate between discouraging and awful. A common error made by novice REFT therapists is to be stumped by the family member's reasoning. Instead, the therapist would do well to realize that the response given is support for a potential rational belief about the situation but not an answer to the original question. The therapist should repeat the question until a more relevant conclusion is arrived at:

T: Of course you'd all feel bad. How is it however that you'd have to see it as much worse than that, utterly awful, as you described earlier?
FM: Because . . . then Dad will be stuck in the same job and keep on with his complaints about being bored and wasting his talents.
T: That may be so and that would be discouraging, but how is that so utterly awful?

FM: The family has been patient with him for a long time and I'm not sure we can be so much longer.

T: That's true that you've all been very patient and it would be sad if your encouragement could not continue as it has. All your responses so far, however, only support why it might be very discouraging if he does not get the promotion, not utterly awful—the end of any possible hope.

FM: Well, although I'm sure we'd be sad, maybe it wouldn't be awful. There's always hope.

Family members will often persist far longer than in this illustration. Therapists' persistence is an invaluable contribution to the use of questioning as a debate strategy.

The second type of cognitive debate is *didactic*, including the use of mini-lectures, analogies and stories. An integral part of the cognitive methodology of REFT is to offer family members corrective information and concepts that will assist them in experiencing more adaptive emotions and considering alternative behavioral solution sequences. REFT therapists regularly discuss with or explain to family members such things as the philosophies of rating versus acceptance, the nature of devastation beliefs, and the potential drawbacks of demandingness.

Lectures are best kept brief and are typically most useful when new ideas are being presented. Used as a part of, or in addition to lectures, analogies and stories offer therapists significant flexibility and creative opportunity to contribute to family members' debates. Stories about other families with similar concerns (disguising identities) and self-disclosure from the therapist's own family life can be employed to illustrate important points. Likewise, analogies abound in the Rational-Emotive literature and REFT therapists typically have developed their own cadre to stress commonly experienced issues.

A third widely used form of cognitive debate is *exaggeration*. Family members often express irrational beliefs without recognizing their relevant impact on their emotions and behavioral solution sequences. Often exaggerating key words and phrases can contribute to family members' debate. For example:

T: "That *must not* happen!" What's the likely impact of such an intense demand on your subsequent actions and feelings versus a more desiring stance expressed by "We don't want that to happen."

A fourth form of cognitive debate is *vicarious modeling*. Therapists can frequently request family members to identify others who have, or are experiencing similar activating events and whose emotional responses and behavioral solution sequences are apparently satisfactory to them. Much can be learned from vicarious modeling. Family members can come to recognize that by not evaluating their own similar circumstances as devastating, others are able to go on with their lives despite unfortunate happenings. This knowledge can be transferred back to themselves. The process can also serve to sensitize family members to look for data in their environment which they may have been selectively screening out. Vicarious modeling is particulary helpful when the A is virtually universal, such as common difficulties presented by developing children and adolescents. Almost all young children attempt to manipulate parents with threats of ". . . then I don't love you!" Likewise, the vast majority of adolescents and their parents have wrestled with "adolescent rebellion" and have managed to do so without experiencing long-term hostility and horror.

Some novice REFT therapists tend to be reluctant in introducing vicarious modeling with families who are experiencing rare or highly aversive activating events (e.g., terminal illness, death of a family member, rape). Family members will often have difficulty debating because of their believing that no one can truly appreciate how traumatic their experience has been. Coping models are available however, particularly in the form of various self-help groups to whom therapists can refer. Walen et al. (1980) offered a clinical example. A mother of a child with Giles de la Tourette syndrome was unfamiliar with the disorder and horrified by her child's bizarre behavior, convinced that her child was the only case in the world so bad. The mother was referred to an association for parents of children with Tourette's syndrome as a concurrent experience coupled with her present therapy. The group provided the mother with coping models; at her next therapy session, she relayed to the therapist, "I guess it isn't so awful . . . people *can* learn to adjust to it."

In essence, general dispute strategies seek to answer two questions relative to family members' irrational and potential rational beliefs: (1) How does it make sense to think . . . ? and (2) How does it help to think . . . ? Walen et al. (1980) proposed that therapists' own grasp of several points for themselves during this process will facilitate family debate. The first of these points concerns the therapist's emphasizing the rational belief about the family's A. How can therapists facilitate family members' debate if they truly believed that the A was *horrible*? If the therapist is not clear in his or her evaluation of the family's A, a personal ABCDEF would be prudent before presenting DEF to the family members.

Another crucial point for the therapist is to be sure that the *right thing* is being debated; that is, the philosophical concept, not the metaphor in which it is expressed. For example, if a parent exclaims "What a jackass I am for having treated the kids that way!" it would be simple to confirm that the parent is clearly not an animal—a jackass. The philosophical concept, however, will have been missed as the parent's irrational belief about human worth being dependent upon accomplishment, in this instance parenting ability, will remain intact.

The therapist had also best recognize that debate can often take a significant amount of time. The same or a similar debate may need to be repeated over the course of many sessions. One way to assure sufficient time for this is to avoid addressing a new problem or prioritized goal in a subsequent session if the family has not finished the process, including E and F, with the issue in question. The next session can begin by the therapist requesting that the family members recall the previous session's discussion, outline that ABC quickly and immediately return to D. A second strategy might be for the therapist to take any new problem raised, suggest how it relates to the family members' basic irrational belief discussed in the previous session, and then proceed with the original debate as a means of dealing with both problems.

A final point is the importance of multiply communicating "stay the same/change/the meaningful new." This reduces possible resistance by working with the family members' motivation. If family members express ambiguity about whether or not they want to change their beliefs, the therapist should refer back to the ABC connection and their previously expressed confirmation that this was an unsatisfactory one. Debate can be hard work for both therapist and family members. Facilitating family members shifting their position on major philosophical issues may require many trials and a good deal of persistence on the part of the therapist. As any effective facilitator, the REFT therapist had better believe in what is being proposed and demonstrate this belief by persistence and enthusiasm for the position— rationality.

DEBATE: SPECIFIC SUGGESTIONS

As indicated in earlier chapters of this book, there are a number of basic irrational beliefs (e.g., "demandingness," "devastation," "discomfort disturbance," and "denigration"). Young (1974, 1983) has made significant contributions in demonstrating "down to earth" challenges in facilitating debate in his work with adolescents. His approach relies primarily on promoting "semantic clarity." It is an approach that provides specific suggestions for facilitating family members' debate in challenging irrational beliefs while simultaneously punctuating their rational counterparts.

1. *Demandingness: "shoulds," "oughts," and "musts."* A significant aspect of family members' irrational beliefs is the tendency to treat wants and desires as if they were absolute rules for living. Many family members typically believe that they must have their way simply because it is deserved, earned, fair, right, just, or whatever. It can be valuable, therefore, to sensitize family members to their personal imperatives and facilitate their understanding how absolutistic thinking usually results only in disturbing emotions and unsatisfactory behavioral solution sequences. Several tactics for accomplishing this end include:

a. Substituting *must* or *demand* for *should* or *ought*. Family members typically use the words should and ought so frequently and indiscriminately that sometimes just getting them to substitute the words must or demand gets the imperative quality across. Once this is established, they tend to find it easier to adopt a more rational, less absolute position.

b. Substituting *absolutely have to* for *should* or *ought*. "We should (or ought to) be able to reach agreement on our major decisions" makes sense to most family members, but "We absolutely have to reach agreement on our major decisions" frequently encourages them to see the disadvantages of maintaining such a belief as well as the advantages of viewing their shoulds and oughts as the more rational *it would be better if.*

c. Substituting *no right* for *should* or *ought*. Another means of expressing the meaning of should used in an absolutistic manner, especially with angry family members, is to exchange "She has no right to do that" for "She shouldn't (or ought not to) do that." The disadvantages of "She has no right" and advantages of maintaining a view of should or ought as conditional is thus often easier to conclude.

d. Offering the *want–need concept*. Another suggestion for facilitating family members' debate is elucidating for them the difference between wanting and needing. Some of the most rigid family members, especially those involved in attempting to solve their concerns through behavioral excesses, are facilitated significantly in critically distinguishing between desires and necessities and using this understanding productively.

e. Showing *demands* as equaling *unbreakable law.* Some family members are facilitated in debate by suggesting that their upsetting emotions and unsatisfactory behavioral solution sequences are significantly contributed to by their belief that their self-proclaimed laws have been broken. "Mother's Commandments have been violated" or "It was Dad's turn to be God, and he got upset because one of the kids broke His rules" are illustrations of this tactic. Once family members grasp the senselessness of their demandingness, it is easier to relate to the idea that they can still desire and work toward achieving their ends even though those ends may not always be realized.

2. *Devastation: "awfuls," "terribles," and "horribles."* A second significant aspect of family members' irrational beliefs is the tendency to blow things out of proportion, to make mountains out of mole hills. The following tactics facilitate family members' debate relative to the sensibility of a more rational belief versus its irrational counterpart.

a. Substituting the words *disaster, catastrophe,* or *tragedy* for *awful, terrible,* or *horrible.* The words awful, terrible and horrible are so much a part of the average family members' working vocabulary that most tend to be very skeptical that the meaning behind these words contributes to their distressful emotions and unsatisfactory behavioral solutional sequences. Family members who strongly hold that their problem is awful are asked, "How is it a disaster?" or "How do you equate it with a tragedy such as . . . ?" These words have a more precise meaning and can be subjected to debate more readily than awful.

b. Using the phrase *end of the world* to suggest to family members that they are exaggerating the "badness" of their experience. Often, family members' initial response to being asked to consider "Would it be the end of the world?" is an eye-rolling "Of course not" which permits the next consideration, "Then exactly what would it be?" The answer, almost always in the realm of a reasonable disadvantage, begins to persuade family members to reevaluate their irrational belief and strongly consider a more rational alternative.

c. Employing the phrase *a fate worse than death.* Once more the use of a familiar, but obviously magnified, term assists family members in debating the disadvantages of their irrational belief versus the greater sensibility of its rational counterpart.

d. Asking, *Could it be any worse?* Often family members exaggerate, considering a situation as totally bad. Encouraging them to consider something that could make their circumstances even worse frequently enables them to decide that it is highly unlikely that any disadvantage (especially their own) is 100% bad. This tactic can sometimes be used in a humorous way by adding different kinds of ridiculous dimensions to their problem situation. This typically aids family members in their debate process by facilitating the consideration that problems are not always as bad as they seem; and by viewing their situation in less exaggerated and more sensible terms, they come to recognize how they may feel much better and consequently address it in a more helpful manner as well.

e. Asking, *What's the worst that could actually happen?* Anxiety-ridden family members' debate process, in particular, can be facilitated in the recognition that they are catastrophizing their complaints by encouraging them to substitute the most realistic but worst outcome they can imagine. This tends to help them stay away from possibilities and to concentrate on actualities. In doing so, family members learn that they'd be better off in dealing with the rational hassle and not the irrational horror of their problem.

3. *Discomfort Disturbance: "I (or we) can't stand it."* A third significant aspect of family members' irrational beliefs is the conviction that they can stand no inconvenience or discomfort. Most family members seem to be able to grasp the disadvantages of "can't stand" beliefs more easily than the other major irrational beliefs as well as be able to positively debate and then adopt more rational counterparts.

a. Substituting *unbearable* for *can't stand.* Family members can often realize how pernicious their can't stands are by equating them with the term unbearable. Hearing things put this way, many family members more rationally conclude, "Well, it's not that bad. I mean I can bear it."

b. Explaining *difficult* versus *impossible.* Frequently, the implications of a can't stand irrational belief can be better grasped by investigating whether a particular problem situation is impossible or is merely difficult to tolerate. Even some of the most rigid family members, in understanding the advantages of this consideration, take on a more rational belief (e.g., "Just because it's a pain in the neck doesn't mean it can't be lived with.").

c. Substituting *won't* for *can't.* Often, when family members repeatedly use the word can't, substituting the word won't is an effective way of facilitating understanding of the contribution of beliefs to solving the problem situation more satisfactorily. It is the belief more than the problem situation itself, that is discouraging a more satisfactory attempt at a solution.

d. Suggesting to the family members that they *are* tolerating the conflict in question. Despite complaints and protests, family members can be reminded that they *have been and are* living with the problem. This tactic is especially valuable with families where there have been long-running problems remaining unsatisfactorily dealt with. For example, the family in turmoil because of an impending divorce characterized by "we just can't stand the hostility" can be facilitated in considering that they have been, in fact, standing the hostility for some time. It may be very uncomfortable to do so, but it need not paralyze their problem-solving capacities.

e. Suggesting that a genuine *can't stand* situation would either end family members' lives or at least render them unconscious. This tactic proposes that if problematic circumstances were so impossible to bear, it would either cost family members their lives or they would very likely pass out from the overwhelming agony involved. And, up to that point, they would be standing the adversity and discomfort; they may not like it, but they would be standing it.

4. *Denigration: self and/or other downing.* This fourth significant aspect of family members' irrational beliefs relates to the disadvantages of global ratings of themselves and others. Its rational counterpart, *acceptance* is one of the most difficult for most family members to adopt, perhaps because comprehension requires a more sophisticated level of understanding.

a. *Using a visual aid.* The therapist draws a large circle and labels it *self*. Next a series of smaller circles is drawn inside the "self" circle. These represent the various traits, characteristics, and performances of the family member(s) in question. Family members are asked to consider if rating one trait or feature as bad makes all of the other circles bad. In essence, family members are facilitated in learning that persons are a collection of qualities, some good and some bad, none of which equal the whole self. Thus, accepting the self, but not necessarily all of the traits is likely to contribute to more helpful emotions and adaptive behavioral solution sequences.

b. *Using an analogy.* Although many examples can illustrate the disadvantages of overgeneralizing from act to personhood, the "flat tire" example is a particularly good one. Family members are asked to consider if they would junk their entire car just because it had a flat tire. The key word is *junk*. Once family members are able to relate to this image, it can be employed as a key to liberally underline the disadvantages of their overgeneralizing mistakes and criticism (e.g., "There you go again, junking your parents because they did such and such").

c. Facilitating the understanding that *although one is responsible for what one does, one is not the same as one does.* This tends to be difficult for many family members to understand. They frequently debate that if someone does something bad, then that person is bad. This can be countered by suggesting they consider, "If you went around mooing like a cow, would you be a cow?" This usually receives a negative reply and can then be followed with "But aren't you saying just that. How come . . . isn't a cow?" With examples offered like this to consider, family members usually begin to separate the act from the person.

d. Explaining *the difference between a person-with-less and less-of-a-person.* Family members experiencing shame, embarassment, or inferiority have usually fallen victim to downing or degrading themselves. To the family members who get criticized or make mistakes, it can be explained that such things prove only that they are persons with less of what they want (e.g., success, approval, etc.), rather than being less of a person. This can sometimes be further illustrated by taking something from them (a shoe, piece of jewelry, etc.) and then asking that they consider, "What are you now? Are you less of a person or just a person with less of what you had?"

e. Suggesting that *blaming is like being punished twice for the same crime.* Particularly with family members who damn themselves and feel excessively guilty, the therapist can ask they consider that mistakes and failings tend to have built-in penalties. Whenever persons err, they not only disappoint themselves and fail to live up to their own standards, but they very likely endure some kind of adverse consequence. Through examples, family members can be helped in considering whether just living with disappointments or negative consequences is punishment enough. Adding to these by denigrating only adds insult to injury and makes moving on to more successful behavioral solution sequences much less likely.

ENACTMENT

When successful at D, family members will have acquired a more rational philosophy relative to A. This more rational philosophy will contribute to emotions that aid effective problem-solving efforts and will be compatible in considering alternative solutions. However, there is still work to be done. REFT holds that unless family members actively put their philosophical restructuring to the test of action, there is little likelihood that second order change has taken place. If two parents were to assert that they "*want*, but don't *have to have* their children immediately obey their requests" yet angrily berate the children when they don't respond right away, the therapist would want to first check whether the most relevant beliefs, rational and irrational, had been adequately debated. If they had, the therapist would want to doubt the conviction of family members' professed rational belief. REFT is not merely a "talk therapy." Once a more rational belief is confirmed, then *enactment* of alternative behavioral solution sequences becomes the next strategic change process.

Enactment begins with family members' realization, "OK, we know the problem, now how are we going to approach it *differently?*" Once recognized and acknowledged, family members are facilitated in *alternative-solution thinking* (Spivack, Platt, & Shure, 1976). This involves *generating* (not merely recognizing) a number of alternative solution sequences. This is akin to the "brainstorming" that was done in assessing and prioritizing their goals at A and that process can be recalled as a model for this Enactment task.

Enactment continues with family members being facilitated in *consequential thinking* (Spivack et al., 1976). This refers to the ability to predict the probable consequences of an alternative solution sequence. The therapist's knowledge of principles of human behavior can provide valuable information in assisting family members in considering possible consequences (Walen et al., 1980). Consider the example of two parents trying to determine how to best deal with their daughter's persistent temper tantrums. Among the alternative solution sequences they generated through brainstorming was ignoring the child when she displayed a temper tantrum (they had previously unsuccessfully demanded she stop, yelling at her to do so). This is the human behavior concept of extinction. The therapist's understanding of this concept allowed the parents to contribute that the immediate effect of this solution might well be an initial increase in the very behavior the parents were seeking to ameliorate. Another contribution the therapist offered was the importance of being very consistent, otherwise, the tantrum behavior might be intermittently reinforced; the therapist further noting that intermittent reinforcement significantly increases a behavior's resistence to extinction, thus prolonging and intensifying it.

Once the family members have evaluated the pros and cons of each of their generated alternative solution sequences, one is prioritized (referring back again to that process undertaken at A) as having the best probability of success. Enactment continues with *means-ends thinking* (Spivack et al., 1976). Family members clarify the sequence of events that will probably occur, identifying the step-by-step sequence required to carry out the alternative solution. The parents in the example above would rehearse exactly how they will implement their extinction plan and how their daughter will likely react, how they will react to her reactions, and so on. As appropriate, role-play and/or actual enactment of the alternative solution sequence would take place in the session.

Another form of enactment herein employed by many REFT therapists is imaginal in the form of *Rational-Emotive Imagery* (Maultsby, 1975; Maultsby & Ellis, 1974). In using this imagery strategy, family members are facilitated in imagining themselves in their problematic A but picturing themselves behaving differently and feeling differently. For example, consider the married couple whose reluctance to assert themselves with the husband's parents has been their unsatisfactory way of dealing with the parents' unreasonable requests.

T: I know the both of you have been having trouble when you think about asserting yourselves with Bob's parents. We've confirmed that a more rational, helpful belief would likely be something like, "We want to show you respect, but this means saying "no" at some times as well as saying "yes" at others." I'd like you both to keep that thought firmly in your consciousness.

C: OK.

T: What I'd ask you to do now is to close your eyes and picture yourselves with Bob's parents. I want you to try to picture yourselves saying to them that you can't come to their place for dinner this Sunday and feeling relatively calm while you're doing it. Bob, you're speaking first slowly and clearly. Karen, you say something to support Bob's "no thanks." Tell me when you get that picture clearly in your mind.

Pause and wait for Bob and Karen's response

C: (Bob nods) Karen: OK.

T: Now what were you saying to yourselves and how were you feeling?

C: Bob: I was thinking "I want to be respectful but this means saying 'no' at times." I felt a bit anxious. Karen: I was thinking a similar thought and I too felt somewhat tense. I was also thinking, however, that I was determined to act assertively, not demanding or giving in, but assertively in a way that shows respect to them but also to us and our desires.

Imagery as in this illustration is most beneficial during Enactment because it allows family members to practice a positive plan and further develop their coping skills.

Enactment concludes with practice of alternative behavioral solution sequences outside of the therapy session. Outside of session, enactments or "homework assignments" generalize the work of therapy beyond the confines of the therapist's office. Homework assignments are thus an essential element of REFT Enactment.

As discussed in Chapter 3, REFT incorporates the MRI theory of change perspective that human problems develop by mishandling of life difficulties. The three basic ways families mishandle those difficulties they encounter include: (1) not taking action when action is necessary; (2) taking action when action is best not taken; and (3) taking action but at the wrong level—the most common form of mishandling that REFT therapists tend to observe. It is important for therapists to continually emphasize that difficulties are not generally mishandled on purpose or for some unconscious gain. Rather, when family members have a problem, they go about attempting to deal with it in a manner that is consistent with their cognitive frame of reference, the B of REFT. Their unsuccessful solutions are maintained because they are considered logical, necessary, or the "only thing to do."

As with Debate relative to family members' beliefs, similarly Enactment entails the therapist being quite clear about what to stay away from; effective enactments are likely to be those in the opposite direction of the family's original thrust. Basing enactment on family members' now more rational frame of reference provides cognitive direction and contributes to an emotional experience compatible with positive problem-solving. The following illustrate common alternative solution sequences frequently found in the practice of REFT at E:

Taking action when action is necessary (as opposed to not taking action when action is necessary). The most common illustration of this occurs when procrastination has been a family's unsuccessful solution. Procrastination almost always involves irrational beliefs about discomfort ("We must be comfortable," "Things should come easy," "It's too hard"). The short-term discomfort of engaging in a task is avoided in spite of the potential longer-term benefit. Almost anything can be the object of procrastination. In the previous section of this chapter, Debate relative to discomfort disturbance beliefs was discussed. In moving to E, family members would best begin with a confirmation of their newly found more rational belief (e.g., "It would be better if disciplining the kids were easier, however, parenting effectively requires experiencing some discomfort"). A beneficial first step is to suggest that family members keep a diary in which they note what they do at times when procrastination has proven an unsatisfactory solution. The diary can help both the therapist and family members get a clear picture from which reasonable behavior changes can be contrasted and agreed to. For example, consider the family in which complaints were coming home from school about the children not completing their homework assignments. The children spent a considerable amount of time talking with their parents at the dinner table after the meal was completed, before beginning their homework. Both the parents and the children previously maintained the irrational belief "It would be too hard to initiate breaking off our after dinner conversations." No action was taken by either when it should have been. At D they confirmed the lack of help this belief afforded them and agreed upon a more rational counterpart that would likely offer them more assistance in contributing to an effective solution ("It is hard to cut short the enjoyment we have socializing after dinner, but this discomfort is necessary if the kids are to do well in school"). An alternative behavioral solution sequence was for the parents to agree to initiate the "end of dinner" sequence at a specific time, the children to agree to thank the parents for their assistance in getting them started on their homework, and the parents to reply with their own thanks to the children for the encouraging comment. Thus, action was taken by all involved, facilitating a more effective solution sequence.

Not taking action when action is best not taken (as opposed to taking action when action is best not taken). Self-indulgence is often a family's unsuccessful solution in situations wherein they are taking action when action is best not taken. Self-indulging behaviors tend to bring momentary, short-term pleasure or relief. While self-indulgence can be a pleasurable part of life, some families habitually and compulsively engage in self-indulgent actions, thus contributing to detrimental long-term results for them. For example, consider the family with a basic irrational belief "Children have to have all their desires met." During D they were facilitated in disconfirming that belief and arriving at the more rational belief "Children's desires are important, but moderation in meeting them teaches patience and cooperation." Emanating from this belief, the therapist promoted the family's enactment of an alternative behavioral solution strategy by teaching them the basics of *response prevention*, that is monitoring and controlling themselves in several ways in order to not take self-indulging action when this action is best not taken. Several of these response prevention strategies include:

Stimulus Control: The family agreed to avoid as much as possible places (e.g., toy stores, candy shops, etc.) where self-indulging actions typically took place.
Reinforcements: The family agreed to indulge only certain pleasures contingent upon refraining from indulging in other circumstances.
Penalties: The family agreed to enact penalities for all should relapse occur.
Substitutions: Harmless enjoyments were devised that the family agreed would be good substitutes for more harmful indulgences.
Physical Distractions: Recreational activities that distracted from the urge to request indulgence by the children and accede to those indulgences by the parents were agreed to. These included board games, walks, etc.

Action is taken on the level most appropriate to the situation (as opposed to action is taken but on the wrong level). This is the most frequent form of mishandling difficulties REFT therapists tend to observe. It is often seen in families making demands as opposed to preferences. A common illustration is one in which a family's unsuccessful solution is one of aggressiveness as opposed to *assertiveness.* Assertive actions, when expressed, derive from family members' *preferences*—they like or do not like something and express that fact. Aggressive actions, when expressed, derive from family members' *demands*—they believe that something *must* or *must not* happen and express that belief. Consider the example of the family wherein parents and teenage children constantly argued over curfew, use of the car, and the like. Both parents and teenagers maintained the irrational belief "You must . . . . " During D they were able to disconfirm the benefits of this belief and affirm the greater utility of a more rational "I or we want . . . ." During E, the therapist assisted the family members in differentiating between assertive and aggressive actions, learning and then carrying out a variety of assertive, as opposed to aggressive, responses for interacting among themselves. These assertive responses included such things as:

1. When expressing a refusal, give a decisive "no"; explain the refusal, but without being unduly apologetic. When possible give those others involved an alternative course of action.

2. Request an explanation when asked to do something you see as unreasonable.
3. When expressing annoyance or criticism, remember: Comment on the *behavior;* avoid personal attacks.
4. When commenting on another's behavior, use "I statements." For example, instead of saying, "You are so unfair!" try, "When the only reply given is a 'No!' I feel stuck." Where possible, offer a suggestion for an alternative action such as "I'd like to see us at least talk a few minutes to better understand each other's point of view before any decision is made."
5. Remember that behaving assertively is no guarantee that you will get what you desire. Assertive behavior does however tend to increase the probability of a favorable outcome.

FEEDBACK

Following enactment, family members move to the final step in REFT's ABCDEF model, that being F or *Feedback.* This is where family members *verify* the effects of their alternative solution sequence. The new solution has been implemented. Its effects are evaluated. How did it work? If satisfactory, self-affirmation is in order (feeding back to A wherein A will no longer be evaluated at B as it was, and so on). If unsatisfactory, the family is led back to A again to begin another ABCDEF (as the feedback to A would be such that at B, the A would still likely be evaluated as it originally was). Feedback basically involves encouraging family members to be scientific in their examination of data and the conclusions they draw from them (Walen et al., 1980).

Good scientists gather data as impartially as possible, attempting to observe and report their observations objectively and accurately. Two primary habits which interfere with scientific data gathering are *selective abstraction* and *magnification/minimization* (Beck, Rush, Shaw, & Emery, 1978). Selective abstraction "consists of focusing on a detail taken out of context, ignoring other more salient features of the situation and conceptualizing the whole experience on the basis of this element" (Beck et al., 1978, p. 7). Magnification/minimization "is reflected in errors in evaluation that are so gross as to constitute a distortion" (Beck et al., 1978, p. 8). In both types of interferences, family members ignore certain features of their circumstances and thus gather biased data. In selective abstraction, family members focus on one category of data only and ignore others; in magnification/minimization, they ignore infor-

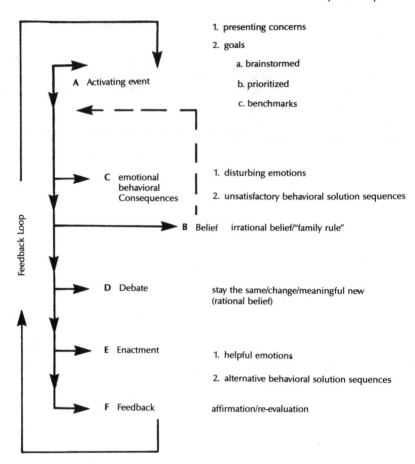

FIGURE 6.1 The ABCDEF of REFT: "Identify A, tie A to C, get B, go to D, tie D to E, move to F, go back to A."

mation within a category. At F the therapist facilitates family members in agreeing on which data are most relevant, thus avoiding selective abstraction. Second, agreeing on one or more members who will keep a log of frequency counts helps avoid the problem of magnification/minimization.

TERMINATION

The family has made progress toward their prioritized goals. There has been second order change in that the rules for governing the system have been altered, evidenced by family members' emotions relative to their As being a degree of intensity helpful to considering and carrying out alternative solution sequences. Said alternative solution sequences have been enacted and then at F affirmed as more successful; feeding back to A wherein A is no longer seen as the problem it was originally. Therapy ends.

The final REFT session is not essentially different from the one before or the ones near the middle of therapy, except for a somewhat greater emphasis on anticipation of future problems and less emphasis on the immediacy of the presenting concerns. In terminating, the family's efforts are given credit for positive change. They are, however, cautioned against thinking that their presenting concerns are resolved forever. The future will hold new and inevitable difficulties. It would be very *irrational* to assume that no further problems will emerge or that they will now always be *totally rational*.

Families who meet the criteria noted above and yet express hesitancy about terminating are facilitated in framing termination as a necessary vacation from therapy, time away from regular therapy providing them an opportunity to incorporate therapeutic gains into their daily life (Segal & Kahn, 1986). Again, the potential adverse effects of trying to become totally rational are referenced. Another appointment might be scheduled in several months for review purposes.

Finally, termination may be approached with mixed emotions by both therapist and family members. The therapist may feel sad about no longer interacting with the family, but also and more importantly, the therapist will experience a sense of satisfaction in the movement that has occurred. The family is also likely to feel sad and a bit apprehensive about the future, but more importantly, pride and confidence that life's difficulties can be dealt with in different ways which lead to greater life satisfaction and goal attainment—rationally.

In terminating this section of the book, Figure 6.1 summarizes the ABCDEF process of REFT. The upcoming Chapters 7 and 8 will offer case studies illustrating how this process comes to life in actual practice.

Part III
Clinical Applications

REFT therapists become involved in families' inter-personal processes (without losing balance nor independence), flexibly supporting and nurturing at one point and challenging and confronting at another.

7

Case Study: "You Have To Understand!"

Having presented the basic features of REFT in the previous chapters, this chapter offers more extensive case material so as to provide a picture of how the ABCDEF process of REFT take place in actual practice. The chapter consists of the verbatim transcription of a tape recorded therapy session. Interspersed among the transcription are comments meant to highlight aspects of the process taking place.

In the following case, the client couple presented as having been married for 1½ years. This is the second marriage for each. Three children are present in the home: the natural child of their present union, a son who is 6 months old; and two other boys (4 years old and 3 years old) who are the natural children of the wife and her former husband. The husband, Doug, reported that he had been unable to "respond well" to his new family milieu. He highlighted his anger and frustration as well as his doubts as to his being the "right person" for his wife. The wife, Carol, reported that there have been significant difficulties for both she and Doug in making necessary mutual marital/family adjustments; these adjustments are compounded by her feelings of discomfort in their present geographic location and Doug's stress relative to turmoil present in his chiropractic practice. Professional assistance was sought with the desire of seeking to make said mutual marital/family adjustments more readily and with less distress.

REFT holds that problems develop primarily through the mishandling of normal life difficulties. For this couple, said difficulties included those mutual marital/family adjustments necessary to the satisfactory evolution of any new marital/family system but particularly more stressful for the second marriage with step-children in the home. Their "difficulties" became problems of a more profound nature when the ways in which they evaluated them became increasingly irrational and subsequently the ways they sought to resolve them did not work. Then, even though said solutions were not working, they maintained their irrational demands and repeatedly employed the same unsuccessful solutions more intensely. Their original "expected" adjustment difficulties became escalated by this vicious-cycle process.

REFT begins by assessing the Activating event, the "A," comprising three major elements: a description of the areas of concern framed as "brainstormed" treatment goals, more specific objectives in the form of "prioritized" treatment goals, and then "benchmarks" that further define the goals in terms of desired outcomes. With regard to this client couple, nine potential treatment goals were brainstormed in the session previous to the transcribed session that follows. From the nine brainstormed goals, three prioritized goals emerged and were confirmed as foci for therapy efforts. These three prioritized goals represent the primary complaints.

The following transcribed session, the couple's third session, begins with a summary of these three priorities and then moves to further define the first of these priorities in terms of desired outcomes or "benchmarks" (i.e., "How will you know when the goal is achieved?"/ primary complaint resolved).

Therapist: T
Carol (wife): C
Doug (husband): D

T: The three goals . . . the first one you identified was for Carol to soften her remarks and Doug not to personalize as much; second was Carol to overcome some of the negative feelings she has toward Doug and Doug not to respond to those so upsettedly; and the last one was for Doug to listen and try to hear Carol more and Carol to offer more benefit-of-the-doubt relative to his having heard her. So if we achieve those three things would you say that your relationship would be enhanced?

D&C: Yes.

T: I assume that the first goal you prioritized would be the one that would be the one most important for you right now or would one of the other two be more important to you?

C: Well, the first one I think . . . is more pressing . . . it's something we keep coming back to . . . .

T: Do you agree?

D&C: Yes.

T: Great. What we want to consider now is "How will you know when you have achieved it?" In other words, what might be something that you will be able to see and say to yourselves "Hey, that says to me that we're at a point where I'm able to soften my remarks more or I'm not personalizing so much," or "She's softening her remarks more or he's not personalizing so much." What might be several events or situations or circumstances that each of you could identify; a couple of benchmarks that would suggest that the goal is being approached if not attained?

(Silence, both Doug and Carol looking in a questioning manner)

T: You can answer that individually. It doesn't have to be something you agree on . . . although it would be nice if you were to agree on what you would see as the benchmarks for this goal.

C: Benchmarks . . . I'm not sure?

T: You might make an educated guess into the future, or another option would be to look into the past when you did handle this difficulty in a way that was satisfying. I'm sure at times it has been worked out OK. But in the future or in the past at those times when it did work out, how did you know that it was OK? What happened. Or what could happen that would say to you "Hey, this is OK." It might be something that you think or feel, something Doug does, you do. . . .

C: Well, sometimes if I'm mad about something that happened during the day and if Doug just says "Oh I know it's tough and you've had a hard day and don't worry about it." That's really all I want is to hear is him say "Oh don't worry about it; it will be better tomorrow" instead of giving me a hard time about it.

T: So, one thing that might be an indication to you, Carol, is that Doug would respond to some of your remarks with a more encouraging stance, a stance implying "It will be better tomorrow."

C: Umhmm.

T: Tomorrow meaning whatever.

T: How will you know Doug?

D: I just think probably . . . I'll be able to recognize the comments she makes won't have some personal connotation attached to them. They'll be more neutral. A lot of times when things do go wrong, either the examples or a part of the expression of dissatisfaction does have something attached to it that does have something to do with me . . . is a more personalized thing.

C: I think that that's the whole problem. It goes back to where we started. I'm saying it doesn't and you say it is . . . that causes problems.

D: No, I'm just saying that they can be phrased differently, but they're not.

C: But when I'm upset and upset about whatever happened, I'm not thinking about how to phrase it so you don't offend the person who is really just more an ear to listen.

D: Maybe I'm a bit off base. . . . A lot of times I'll have a long day or a bad day . . . .

T: What you are saying is fine. It doesn't have to be qualified. What I heard you identify was that if Carol's remarks don't seem so personal, to have that personal connotation attached to them, that would be an indication to you that you were achieving that goal.

D: Maybe I could rephrase it. I feel it will be easier to recognize when the timing . . . a lot of times she'll hit me with these problems that happen during the day while I'm getting out of the car in the garage or as soon as I walk in the door instead of allowing me to change clothes and relax.

C: How are you going to recognize that as a benchmark? If I don't say anything, does that mean that nothing happened or is that going to mean that I'm holding off saying something?

D: I'm not talking about not saying anything at all or doing it hours later, but instead of meeting me at the door and being all wound up about the problem. . . . I've just finished a long day . . . give me a few minutes to catch my breath when I come home, and then come to me. I think I would recognize that. Most of the things I can think of that were problems or have been problems in the past have been things that . . . it's just been bad timing. I could be wrong.

T: There's not a right or wrong there. What we're saying is that this is something that you would be able to use as a benchmark for yourself. For example, your part of that goal, Carol, is to soften your remarks more. . . . Doug perceives the remarks to be softened by being approached at another time than when he first comes home from work; not that the remarks themselves would be any different, but that they would be perceived as softer if approached at a different time. I could see that as a benchmark.

D: By different time, I don't mean like a 24-hour period or waiting 'til the weekend, but just . . . maybe just a few minutes, or at the dinner table instead of immediately upon entering the door. I can see her point too. It will be easier since she's the one, since the goal is on her making a remark and me not taking it so personally. It's much easier for her to recognize what she's doing, her part of it than for me to recognize what I perceive as a benchmark.

T: But by the same token, it might be easier for you not to personalize it as much if it's not approached when you come home . . . right away. We don't want to discount what you perceive as a benchmark, we can come back and change them. But would you see that as a possibility for yourself, would you say "Hey, it looks like the goal is being more closely attained" if that was to occur?

D: Umhmm.

T: What else might you use as a benchmark relative to Carol—you softening your remarks more and Doug, you not personalizing as much? The things you identified already are very good benchmarks. What else might you use? What would you like to see Doug do? Doug, what would you like to see Carol do?

(Silence, Carol particularly looking quizzically)

T: Are you having a hard time identifying these things?

C: Benchmarks? Yeah. I guess if we could identify those, maybe we wouldn't be here.

T: Well, it's a good indication of why it's important to identify them; hopefully it will help you feel a little more patient as we seek to struggle with them because if we don't have these benchmarks, then it's going to be difficult to have anything for you to grasp hold of and say "Hey, I think we're where we want to go."

C: Right, that's what I was saying. If I don't say anything, how are you really going to know. How are you going to know if I'm getting better . . . only by what I'm saying, or is it just that I didn't think about saying it; or it wasn't an intense enough feeling.

D: No, that's what I'm saying. I'm not saying not to say it.

(Both Doug and Carol speak simultaneously)

D: As far as not taking it personally; so much of that has to do with what kind of day I've had. If every little thing has seemed personal during the day and with what I do it is very personal. If I've had one of those days where everything is . . . I've heard lots of complaints and lots of little problems, it's going to be more difficult to take it and to be more relaxed about what you say than it would be if everything went fine.

C: OK. Then how about this: Why don't you give me a call before you come home and say "I've had an especially bad day today" . . . to warn me. Then I won't jump on you as soon as you walk in the house.

T: It's a great idea. What I'm asking you to do though is to hold off on the possible solutions for now. It's a good solution and you might want to consider it. If we could just try and focus on how we will know right now. One thing to think about is that a lot of how you'll know is by how you perceive it.

C&D: Right.

T: You may be quiet and still mad or you may be quiet and happy as can be; depending upon how it is perceived determines the benchmark . . . the situation could be totally opposite to how it's perceived so we might want to look at perceptions as well as actual events too. Something to think about. You might want to look at benchmarks as also how you think about things too.

C&D: Umhmm.

T: What else would you want to see? How else would you know that he wasn't personalizing so much? Can you think of an example where Doug has personalized recently? Maybe that might help us. And Doug if you can think of an example where you felt that Carol's remarks were too harsh and then we could look at what scenario you would have liked to have seen instead, and that might give us some more benchmarks.

C: I can't think of anything specific really.

T: There have got to be hundreds of them.

C: I know.

D: The one that I think of is the one with the photographs the other day.

T: How about for you Doug? How did you see yourself personalizing there or Carol coming forth with harsher remarks?

D: Well, as far as the harshness of the remark . . . I take a lot of photographs.

T: That's your hobby.

D: Sort of. I do it in the office also. As I was trying to take this picture . . . her comment . . . she didn't want me to take it right then until she got the kids changed and the comment I guess I took the wrong way was that she was tired of all these yucky photographs, yucky pictures. I guess I took offense to it. I thought that she had perceived that I had been taking . . . was not pleased with a lot of . . . the pictures I had taken lately. I guess I was offended by that.

T: Did she say or did you understand her to imply that she was tired of the pictures?

D: Well, just by saying I'm tired of all these yucky pictures.

T: That's what she actually said.

D: Yeah.

T: I'm just trying to understand what went on.

D: I think that was pretty much it.

T: That was verbalized, not something that you just perceived as being implied.

D: No, it was verbal . . . a specific thing said that she didn't like.

T: What would you have liked to see there? We don't have to pursue that any further other than the fact of . . . what would you have liked to see there in terms of this goal? If Carol could have . . . let's assume that she was not desirous of taking more pictures; I'm not saying that you weren't. Let's just assume that for a second. How would you have liked her to phrase that? Maybe, don't take their pictures right now. The kids look terrible. Take the pictures after . . .

         (Both Doug and Carol speak simultaneously)

C: That was the first time. I wanted to change their clothes. And then I said enough . . .

D: Well, I guess my perception was that it was just a Polaroid. What I do is 35 millimeter and I was just going to take a snapshot just for them to view. I was just going to snap one because the kids are fascinated with pictures and I was just going to let them take that one . . . and so my desire was not to set this up and take and show the office and so why not just go and take this picture . . .

C: See that's what I mean. He thinks I'm talking about his yucky photography. I'm talking about the kids looking crummy and their crummy clothes.

T: I would ask you think in your own minds "Why do I need to defend myself right now?" I'm sure that there's times you want to defend yourself, but right now? Could we just let it go for the moment? In that situation what would you have liked to see, not why did it happen or what were the facts of the matter but what would you have liked to see Carol do? And I'll ask you Carol the same question.

D: I guess let me take the picture, just go ahead and snap it.

T: And so in a more general sense, how might you phrase that as a bench-mark? For her to be more accommodating to some of your desires?

D: I don't know if it's so much that . . . she always wants everything to be perfect . . . so even for snapshots she likes everything to be perfect.

T: So maybe if . . . a benchmark might be if you were able to perceive Carol's desires for things to be perfect, as you describe it, for that not to come across as much; for her to be more willing to go along with imperfection. Would that be a benchmark for you?

D: Yeah. But I'm sure that in her mind she feels like she does that all the time. It's impossible with three kids to have everything perfect.

T: What we're talking about is your perception. It's a matter of how you see it.

D: OK.

T: How about you Carol, in that situation if we could use that, or if you have another situation we could use, what would you have liked to see happen . . . from Doug's standpoint?

C: I think that I would have liked for him to just . . . since he was snapping the pictures, to just go along with what I said. I said I wanted to put a new shirt on him. It would only take five minutes to put a clean shirt on him. He could have said "How long is it going to take?"

T: What did you see him personalize there?

C: That he was saying that I was saying that he was a terrible photographer and all we get are a bunch of terrible yucky pictures.

T: What part of that would you like to see different?

C: Well, I'd like him to realize that I wasn't talking about the photography. I was talking about the subjects of the photograph which were the kids in crummy clothes.

T: So maybe if Doug took a more total view of your comments rather than trying to hone in on one little part.

C: Right. How it affects his part . . .

T: Would that be a possible benchmark? If he took a view of how it affected the total picture rather than just him? Would that say to you "Hey, I think this goal is being achieved?"

C: Yes.

T: So, Carol, the goal being for you to soften your remarks somewhat and Doug, for you to not personalize as much. Carol, you'll know that that goal is being moved toward when Doug is able to respond with a more supportive stance to things that happen . . . implying it will be better tomorrow, and also if Doug will take a more total view rather than just how the situation affects him. Then you'd know that you're moving in the right direction.

C: Yes.

T: Doug, you said that you would know . . . if Carol's remarks were better timed, for example, if she had something of concern to address and not do it right when you walked in the door; and the other thing that she would be more accepting of imperfection. How does that sound?

The "benchmarks" having been determined, the three elements of the Activating event are therein identified and clarified. Since REFT sees problems as persisting in part because of the unsuccessful efforts of family members to solve them, the next step involves obtaining an understanding of how said problems have been behaviorally dealt with and the emotional accompanyment to those dealings. This involves assessing the behavioral and emotional Consequences relative to the Activating event: the A–C Connection. The following portion of the session addresses this.

T: I cannot imagine that you haven't already made significant efforts to achieve the goal we are addressing here; you may not have identified it as concretely as we have but it doesn't appear that you've been unaware of it. That goal is one I'm sure you have been working towards in different ways. What have been the ways that you've sought to achieve it so far? I'm sure that you have tried to get Doug not to personalize so much and I'm sure that you've tried to get Carol to soften some of her remarks . . . and at times maybe you've been successful but apparently not over a long enough time or not successful often enough.

C: I don't think that he does . . . try to get me to soften my words. He just, if I say something, he'll say "You don't need to talk to me so mean; don't be so mean to me. I didn't deserve to be talked to like that." And that just puts me on the defensive.

D: I try not to take things so personally. I just ignore a lot of the things . . . a lot of the remarks.

T: Let me back up for one second. Carol mentioned that sometimes what you do is tell her not to talk so harshly. Is that something that you see yourself as having done?

D: Yes.

T: Tell Carol not to be so harsh . . . and the other thing you do at times or have tried is to just ignore.

D: A lot of the times she's complaining about things . . . I just don't say anything.

T: So you take it to extremes. Can you think of any other ways you've tried to get Carol to soften her remarks? Those are probably the two most common ways of doing it but maybe you've also tried some other ways as well . . . think about it for a second.

D: OK.

T: Carol how about you. What have you done to get Doug not to personalize so much?

C: Tell him not to take it so personally or I'll try to explain what I really meant by what I said.

T: Have you also tried to ignore him?

C: No. I don't think so.

T: Anything else?

C: Usually I explain; or I get angry instead of just ignoring it.

T: You do walk away though.

(Both Doug and Carol speak simultaneously)

D: I guess in a way that's kind of not responding or ignoring it.

T: What do you think Carol? How do you see yourself?

C: The only reason I usually walk away is when things get volatile; when things get to where everybody's yelling and . . . it's out of hand; that's why I walk away.

T: That's something that you've tried though.

C: Yes . . . what we're talking about is the little arguments about taking something personally. It's not really the same situation as I see it.

T: So one thing that you've done is to tell him not to take it so personally and the other thing, which is probably harder, is to explain what you really meant.

C: Umhmm.

T: Anything else that you've tried? Anything real creative or unique? And again, these are two excellent ways of responding. . . . Can you think of anything though?

C: No.

T: Doug, how about you?

D: No.

T: I assume that telling Carol not to be so harsh and ignoring her, not saying anything, has not been effective for you. Are you still doing these things?

D: I don't think I tell her many things . . . recently, it's been my habit not saying anything.

T: Is that working for you?

D: Sometimes.

T: How does that work for you? And when I say you, I mean you as an individual, but also you as a couple?

D: I guess it really doesn't . . . we argue . . . as a couple, personally I think it does work sometimes because I've got more important things to worry about. The problem is forgotten but ultimately some of the other things that I think about us falling back to aren't lost so easily and I guess I internalize my feelings. They come back when stress gets built up.

T: And so while telling her not to be so harsh and ignoring sometimes help in the short term, it sounds like they come back to haunt you. It also sounds like the feelings you experience are awfully intense at times, your internalized stress, I assume, is anger and frustration.

D: I'd say that's correct.

T: And so would you say that that's really working for you all?

D: No, I don't think it's . . . if it lingers.

T: How about you Carol, telling Doug not to take things so personally, has that been effective for you?

C: Well, to a certain degree it is because when I say that, he does sometimes listen to what I'm saying, what I'm pointing out. So in a way, it does work.

T: I'm hearing a "but" there somewhere.

C: Well, but then he often ends up feeling mad and resentful about it later on so that's not good . . . and I get very upset when he starts bringing up what I thought was past.

T: So, in the short term again, as with Doug's solutions, it sounds like it has some beneficial effects but over the longer haul it doesn't seem like it's a real helpful thing for your relationship.

C: No.

T: What about explaining to him what you really meant?

C: That does occasionally work . . . he doesn't . . . well, for instance, the picture . . . he doesn't really . . . I don't know if he really believed my explanation . . . I don't know if he's got it in his head that if it's one way maybe he just took it a little bit too personally and that's the end of it . . . because he says to me "You didn't hear how you sounded." I don't know that my explanation really counts . . . . I don't think he really believes . . . . I think he thinks the explanation is more a coverup than an explanation. I really get very upset at times over this.

Although family members may try a variety of problem-solving attempts, there is usually a common denominator, a belief or "family rule" that appears to guide these problem-solving efforts. REFT posits that it is the irrational beliefs that family members hold about the Activating event that contribute to unsuccessful behavioral solution sequences and disturbing emotions at C. The following session portion involves assessing and confirming the couple's irrational "family rule."

T: We've noted earlier the importance of your perceptions, your thinking about each other's intentions as well as actions. There's one thing I keep hearing here as an overriding rule relative to the goals and solutions that you've tried out. It sounds to me, and this is a hypothesis . . . that each of you is thinking something like "He or she should understand me, especially my intentions." What do you think about that?

C: I think that's right. In fact, he's told me that. He hasn't told me that lately, but that's what he used to tell me.

D: I think there are certain things . . . I do get the feeling that there are certain areas that are not as big a priority to her as they are to me . . . .

T: When Carol made the comments about the pictures, what was your thought there relative to how much she was understanding your intentions?

D: Well, she's very quality-oriented, perfection-oriented, and I guess a lot of the problems have to do with my feelings that a lot of the things I do, and I avoid doing a lot of things now that I didn't before because I know they're not going to be accepted well, it gets so frustrating when she interprets wrongly . . . doesn't understand my actual intent.

T: So your thought is "She ought to understand better and just let more things pass"; perhaps even stronger "She has to understand!"

D: Yeah . . . my perception is that her striving for that perfection and that everything to be just so outweighs my feelings about . . . it's more important for it to be a certain way . . . just so . . . that's more important than my feelings . . . I get mad when I even just think about it.

T: Carol, you identified that belief as something you see Doug as thinking. How is it for you? How do you see that rule operating for you in the interactions between you two?

C: I just don't think that things that he gets his feelings hurt about is an indication of how much I understand . . . because if he understood them as I intended them, he wouldn't get his feelings hurt.

T: So what are you saying about your part in that? I hear you thinking to yourself "I care a lot . . . Doug ought to understand that" and perhaps like Doug's thinking much of the time, you too often think even more intensely "He must understand!"

C: Umhmm . . . . That's been my argument all along . . . complaining about me not showing enough affection . . . it always boils down to . . . he basically ends up telling me "You don't understand me" when it's him that doesn't understand, and that makes me feel mad . . . he doesn't recognize my feelings . . . .

T: And he must!

C: Right.

T: And so it seems to be relatively clear that you both are operating much of the time under the belief that "He or she must understand me and my intentions!" Can you see how having this thought so often in the forefront of your mind contributes to the anger and misery you both are experiencing as well as to repeating the same generally unsatisfactory solutions to deal with the problems you note . . . particularly not being able, Doug, to facilitate Carol's speaking less harshly, and Carol, you to facilitate Doug's not personalizing so much.

C: Umhmm.
T: Doug, what do you think about that?
D: Yeah. It sure seems that way to me . . . .

REFT posits that once family's members basic irrational rule relative to their Activating event is determined, treatment moves from assessment to strategic change processes. The client couple's A, C, and B offer direction regarding what might be done to resolve their primary concern/achieve their goal. Initially this entails understanding those strategic change processes to be avoided; that is, those interventions that would simply be a variation of the client couple's attempted solutions, particularly their basic rule. REFT proposes that interventions be identified which represent movement 180° or some variation therein in the opposite direction. The D of REFT, Debate, seeks to facilitate movement from a basically irrational rule to a more rational one relative to the couple's first prioritized goal. Debate begins by introducing cognitive dissonance with regard to the couple's irrational rule by presenting the rational counterpart to that irrational rule relative to their first prioritized goal in a manner that says to them "Stay the same." Debate proceeds with the further communication "But change." "The meaningful new" is then provided by focusing on the value of debating the sensibility and helpfulness of each, the irrational and rational rules, in contributing to more satisfying emotions and successful behavioral solution sequences. Debate concludes with a confirmation of the benefits of adopting the more rational operating rule.

T: I want to express some agreement with both of you relative to your basic operating rule. Your desire to have each other understand your intentions is an important one. It makes for a good relationship. My concern, however, is that you all too frequently move past that desire to a demand that "He or she must absolutely understand my intentions!" How realistic is it, Doug, to think that Carol absolutely has to understand your intentions?
D: It's not realistic and that's part of the reason we're here . . . because you know, when she doesn't understand I get frustrated and angry. I know that I can't force her to understand but at times I find myself compelled to get through to her and it's incredibly frustrating.
T: It's not realistic, and by the same token, how helpful is that demanding belief . . . the one that contributes to that incredibly frustrating feeling and to solutions such as unsuccessfully telling Carol that she has to understand or resentfully ignoring her?

D: Obviously, it's not helpful but I'm at a loss at what else to do.

T: We'll come back to what to do in a moment. Carol, what about you? How realistic do you see that operating rule you both adhere to? "Doug absolutely must understand my intentions!"

C: When you state it that way . . . it would be OK for him not to understand about my makeup or my figure or anything like that but there are certain more serious issues I think it is realistic to expect him to better understand.

T: Might you give me an example?

C: Well, for example, my first marriage and divorce. There are things that are important to me for him to recognize. I've told him many times, but I feel like he just doesn't understand.

T: And it's realistic to expect that he absolutely has to!

C: Not absolutely has to, but I sure want him to.

T: Of course you want him to and that's where we want to go . . . to desire he understand and work to contribute to his doing so. But we'll get back to that thought in a moment. How helpful has it been to demand he understand, considering the solutions of repeatedly unsuccessfully explaining your intentions and/or telling him not to personalize?

C: Those solutions haven't changed things much.

T: And what about the anger and frustration that accompanied those solutions?

C: There're just not right . . . full of tension.

T: You both were relatively clear in noting that you want, you'd like each other to understand your intentions. You also noted, however, that your demanding as opposed to wanting or liking is both unrealistic and not very helpful in considering the type of solutions the demands have contributed to. How realistic and helpful would it be, Doug, if you didn't demand but rather desired that Carol understood your intentions?

D: It would be more realistic because I obviously haven't been able to force her understanding. As far as helpful . . . .

T: For example, if you weren't demanding she understand your intentions but rather desiring she understand which carries the implication that she may not at times . . . might it have been easier to recognize that she possibly was not downing your photography in the situation we discussed earlier, but rather making a comment relative to what the kids were wearing?

D: Yeah, I guess so.

T: Or even if she was actually downing your photography for some unknown reason, might it have possibly been easier to not personalize it if you were desiring she understand your intentions but recognize that this means there will be times she may not.

D: I see what you're saying. Yeah.

T: Carol, the same for you. If you were able to think to yourself "Although I'd like Doug to understand my intentions, it's unrealistic and not very helpful to think that he absolutely has to. I want him to though, but this means there may be times he won't understand my intentions," how might you see yourself less upset and/or acting differently?

C: If I was able to think that?

T: If you were able to have that "desiring" as opposed to "demanding" operating rule consciously in the forefront of your mind you'd feel and likely act how?

C: Well, I'd be more patient with Doug's not understanding and I'm sure I wouldn't get angry with him. I'd still want him to come to understand better my intentions at some point though.

T: Of course you would, and given your mutual ability to maintain the more realistic and helpful operating rule we've just noted, let's consider how we might facilitate that understanding in a more satisfying and successful manner.

Successful at Debate, the couple has acquired a more rational operating rule relative to their first prioritized goal at A. This more rational rule will contribute to emotions that aid effective problem solving efforts and thus be compatible with considering alternative solutions. Enactment is the next strategic change process, wherein alternative behavioral solution sequences are generated, their potential consequences considered, and then planned and carried out. As with strategic change relative to the couple's basic irrational belief during Debate, initiating Enactment involves first considering what to avoid; that being alternative solutions that are simply a variation of the couple's already unsuccessfully attempted solutions. REFT recommends alternative solutions 180° or some variation therein in the opposite direction of the unsuccessful solutions.

T: Carol and Doug . . . the rule of thumb in looking at different solutions when the ones we've tried haven't been satisfactory enough is to consider what would be 180° in the opposite direction or some variation therein. Carol, what would be 180° in the opposite direction of telling Doug not to personalize or explaining to him what your intentions are?

C: Not telling him or explaining . . . but even with the new operating rule, I still want him to understand.

T: OK. You're right and I'm impressed with your confirmation of that "desiring" operating rule. Maybe we don't want to move a total 180° but only a variation therein. Doug, what about you? What might you see as some variation toward the opposite direction of telling Carol not to be so harsh or ignoring her remarks while desiring that she understand you?

D: Maybe if I would try to understand her more rather than trying to get her to understand me so much.

T: A great idea! How might you see that Carol?

C: It's something I haven't done much of lately, that's for sure.

T: With your common operating rule being a demanding one, demanding that the other person understand you, it is pretty clear that it would be unlikely that either of you would have considered how you each might work at understanding the other better. Thus, what you've done is to tell, explain, or ignore. I never really heard where either of you has spent much time listening . . . . That demanding rule leads to a strong offensive position of "You understand me!" whereas a desiring rule tends to lead to a more nurturing position of "Let me understand you, let me hear you so that then maybe I can facilitate your understanding me better." What do you think would be the consequences of allowing yourselves to sit back and listen more to each other?

(Silence, both Carol and Doug appear to be considering the question.)

T: Can you remember a time or times, Carol and Doug, where you, Doug, felt that you were just able sit back and listen to Carol and Carol you just being able to sit back and listen to Doug?

C: No, I don't remember . . . .

D: Not exactly . . . .

C: It's difficult at times . . . because a lot of times the kids are around and so it's impossible to stop and just listen because there are so many external stimuli . . . .

D: The kids especially take so much of our time.

T: I'd assume that one or both of you were raised in environments in which you were taught to tell more than listen or speak more than listen and that's beneficial at times . . . again the solutions that you both utilize are what would normally work . . . if they have somebody who can listen to them. I would assume you have . . . when you first met each other and just talked about yourselves, and Carol you just spoke about yourself and Doug, you just sat there and listened and obviously interacted with her but didn't say a whole lot, instead tried to understand what was being said, and vice versa. Let's say, for example, when my wife and I first met and she was sharing with me about her days at South Broward High School, I didn't say to her "That was ridiculous; how could you be childish?" I'd just sit and listen to her and sort of enjoy what she had to say; it was interesting to me because I wanted to know and understand her better. But you've done that before. What's that experience like for both of you as you remember it?

D&C: It was nice.

T: That might be a direction we want to start with. There's an exercise that's called the "Marriage Conference" that I'd like to suggest for you, at least in the interim until we get together next. Basically, what it involves is putting aside . . . and this is somewhat exaggerated and artificial. What it involves is setting aside a half hour. For half that time . . . flip a coin to decide who goes first . . . for the first 15 minutes, let's say Carol, if you win the toss so to speak, just talk about yourself and Doug is to sit there and listen with no feedback at all and just tries to understand you better. At the end of the 15 minutes, then Doug you spend the 15 minutes just talking about yourself and Carol listens and tries to understand you better. It's something that will help you both carry out your new operating rule "I want him or her to understand me better." Keep that rule consciously in the forefront of your mind and should the old demand re-emerge ask yourself how realistic and helpful that thought is and what would be more realistic and helpful. I also think you'll find you'll feel a lot closer just by listening. I know that a half hour out of your day might be a lot of time for you. I'm not suggesting every day, maybe every other day 'til we meet together next? Is that something that you might be able to start out with? Be sure. If you commit to it, I'd ask you to be sure. If we make a commitment, it is important that we follow through.

C: Umhmm.

D: That's fine.

T: You may want to decide upon a specific time to spend given the concerns you raised earlier about the kids and the like.

C: What about right after we put the kids to sleep?

D: It's probably the best time.

T: Can we begin tomorrow evening and then every other night right after you put the kids to bed until we meet next?

D&C: Yeah.

Following Enactment, the final step in REFT's ABCDEF model is Feedback. This is where the couple verifies the effects of their alternative solution sequence. The new solution has been implemented. Its effects are evaluated. For this couple at this time, feedback will initially occur outside of the therapy session to be followed up on and reaffirmed if successful or reevaluated and recast in a new ABCDEF if evaluated as unsatisfactory during the next therapy session.

T: One final request. After each "Marriage Conference" time you hold, I'd ask that you each take just 5 minutes or less and fill out these "How My Marriage Conference Went" sheets. As you'll notice there are four columns. Just make a few brief comments in completing the sentence noted in each column. "I'm thinking . . . ," "I'm feeling . . . ," "I learned . . . ," and "Congratulations because . . . or I'm going to do this differently next time . . . ." Don't share them with each other til we meet next time. We'll share your responses at the beginning of our next session. Any questions?

D&C: No.

T: Could we end by my asking you two to talk together and summarize what you've experienced during our session time today and what you will do during the interim at home before our next session.

This transcribed session encompasses REFT's ABCDEF process in action for the client couple's first prioritized treatment goal. Future sessions would continue to address this first goal and then would sequentially address their other two prioritized goals similarly, as needed.

8

Case Study: "It's Too Hard!"

Rational-Emotive Family Therapy is first and foremost a way of thinking about families; it is not necessarily associated with a specific set of techniques. The REFT therapist has several general tasks to perform relative to the ABCDEF process, however, each of these elements can be attended to in a variety of ways with a great number of techniques. The selection of techniques will be influenced by a number of factors, including the following: how the therapist's personal style blends with REFT theoretical concepts, the characteristics of the present family system, the personalities of the individual family members, the nature and severity of the presenting problem/therapeutic goals, the particular family members present, and the context in which the therapy occurs.

The uses of REFT treatment are as diverse as the therapeutic techniques that might be employed. There are no hard and fast rules governing the length or number of sessions. The duration and scheduling of sessions depend upon such variables as the therapist's style, the phase of therapy, the nature and severity of the presenting problem/ therapeutic goals, etc. Therapy may take anywhere from one session to many sessions that might span several years.

Chapter 7 presented a case study that might be characterized as "by the book" REFT. This chapter similarly consists of the verbatim transcription of a tape recorded therapy session. Again interspersed in the transcription are comments to highlight aspects of the process taking place. This case differs, however, in being more illustrative of a "flexible and creative" REFT.

The case study emanated from an REFT training seminar conducted by one of the present authors. Part of said seminar was a demonstration session with a volunteer family, neighbors of one of the seminar sponsors. The contract with the "client" family was to participate in a one-session demonstration and a telephone follow-up two weeks later. Particularly given the time-limited aspect of the therapy demonstration, the therapist sought to quickly hypothesize à la REFT theory, and then readily act upon those hypotheses. Family member interaction within the session was highlighted in constantly accumulating new information to confirm and/or revise said hypotheses.

Therapist: T
Joan (mother): J
Roy (father): R
David (son, age 8): D

T: We've got about 45 minutes today and one thing I'd want to highlight again is that the session we are having today is a one-time session. We will, as agreed, have a telephone follow-up in a week or two. At that time we could, however, discuss a referral to someone on staff here at the Center for continuing therapy should you see the value in that option at that time. I initially want to thank you for your willingness to participate and hope that both you and the seminar participants will benefit significantly from the experience. Why don't we begin by Roy, you, or Joan giving me some kind of idea of what you'd like to gain from our session time today.

R: One of the things that I would like is the understanding of what causes the difficulties David is experiencing in school.

T: I'm going to take some notes but I'll be listening while you're speaking.

R: OK. David is in second grade again this year, he's started out doing very poorly; not poorly as in bad grades, but poorly as in completing work. He'll come home with little or no work completed during the day and after conferences with teachers and and the like, we feel we've exhausted our own resources and just find we're unable to motivate him.

T: How about you Joan . . . what would you like to gain from our session time today?

J: Well, I am just about at my wits' end . . . we know that David is smart and we know that he can do the work . . . and we've just tried everything we know to get him to see the seriousness of getting his work done in school rather than bringing it home and I get home at four o'clock and he's been having to do all the work that he didn't do in school in addition to his homework . . . and I come in at four o'clock after teaching all day and have to then push and nag and get him to get on with the work and it takes up all his free time . . . I want him to have free time to play but even more so, I can't stand not having free time for myself after work. I've tried setting a clock. I've tried talking to him. I've tried helping him. I've tried leaving him alone. I just don't know what to do. I'm exasperated.

T: So David's not doing well in school, but it sounds like you are extremely frustrated too, as well as his not doing well in school. Roy, I didn't seem to sense as much frustration from you as Joan?

R: I'm not too concerned as far as that. I am concerned though that if it continues the way it is, it could lead to more serious problems.

T: So you see that as something more in the future as opposed to something in the present.

J: It's certainly presenting a problem for me right now . . . every day, the same thing. I've just had enough.

T: David, did your parents explain to you why we're here today?

D: No.

T: Do you have any idea why we're here?

D: No.

T: Could I ask you to ask your dad or mom to explain to you why we're here together today.

D: OK. Daddy why are we here?

R: Well, we would like to have an understanding about how to help you . . . how to help us to encourage you to do your schoolwork and completing tasks . . . and finishing things. I guess that's it.

D: You want me to do my work?

R: Yes.

D: I am doing my work.

R: Well, how come your teachers keep sending notes home to us that you're not?

D: Well, it's too hard Daddy.

R: When you do your work, you do it well and get good grades . . . I really don't think that that's a reason . . .

J: Listen David, this is serious business. We need to . . . I did tell you we were coming in order to solve a problem that we keep fighting over every day. We have the same fights when I get home and at home it's the same thing . . . you have not been doing your work in school and then you have to bring it home. . . .

D: But I do my work Mom.

J: But that's at home . . . in school you have not been completing your work. We get the notes every day that say you don't do your work. And then all that work has to be done in addition to your homework and there's no time left over for you or me! In addition . . .

D: Mom, you're hurting my feelings.

J: Well, I'm not really meaning to hurt your feelings but this is kind of a serious problem that we need to take care of.

T: Joan, you mentioned that you're oh so frustrated with what's going on and it's nice of you to try to help out Roy in explaining to David the reason we're here together. Why don't you take a break for a second . . . you've been working real hard . . . let Roy try and follow up on what he started. David, would you tell your father why you now think he wants you to be here today.

D: Daddy, you want me to do my work, but I am doing my work.

R: David!
T: It doesn't sound like you are all clear on this, particularly David. Roy, might you try a bit more to help him understand a bit better why we're together here today. It still seems somewhat confusing to him by what he's saying . . . that you want him to do his work, but he sees himself as doing it.
R: I'm not sure either, and I guess that's maybe why we're really here.

In this initial interaction, the therapist makes some initial hypotheses to himself relative to the family's A, B, and C. The A, he sees as David's difficulty in school, particularly completing his work in school. The C, he views as Joan's frustration and unsuccessful prodding of David, as David's frustration and unsuccessful prodding of himself. The C relative to Roy is still somewhat unclear as he presented as relatively disengaged. The therapist facilitated his engagement with David in the session by asking Joan to "take a break" from her hard work to try to better ascertain his part of the C. Roy's frustration with trying to explain to David becomes evident as is his too unsuccessfully utilizing "prodding" to occasion understanding. The common B at this point appears to relate to a core "discomfort disturbance" contributing to an "It's too hard" operating rule being held by all. The therapist then seeks to generate more information to test these hypotheses.

T: We've generated some general ideas about what you all would like to see happen in today's session. If you had to pick one specific goal . . . you mentioned understanding, motivating David . . . we really only have time to address one goal. . . . What might that be?
R: I think that a very good goal would be understanding.
T: How about you Joan . . . what would you like that goal to be?
J: I'd think I would like to know some things to do that are different from what I'm doing every day when we come home . . . it seems to me that we jump around trying to do different things and sometimes opposite things and we're not sure . . . I'm not sure which things work and which things don't work and I think maybe . . . and finally I'm so frustrated, I just get angry and David gets upset and we just . . . the issue just doesn't seem to be resolved.
T: It sounds like you see David as being very frustrated too.
J: Yes. Certainly when I get very frustrated and angry, he gets upset and his feelings are hurt . . . but I get upset because I'm so frustrated because I know he can do the work and be more independent and I just don't think I should have to be helping him as much as I have to.
T: And so David being more independent would be the goal of your choice.
(Joan nods affirmatively)

T: David, is there anything that you would want? Your parents might act differently or you might act differently in some way . . .

D: I'd like them to play with me more.

T: Great.

D: I don't know why Mom gets so mad at me.

T: So your goal might be for them to play with you more or for Mom not to get so mad at you. Anything else?

D: No.

T: Thanks a lot for sharing. You all identified great goals, but as I mentioned earlier, we'll only have time for one today. Let me just summarize the ones you each noted and then I'd ask that you talk among yourselves and agree on one of those in the next few minutes . . . Roy, you proposed achieving greater understanding of what is going on with David. Joan, you proposed achieving ways to deal better with the frustrations that are being experienced and for David to be more independent. David, you proposed that you'd like to see you all play together more and for Mom not to get so mad. Would the three of you talk about and come to an agreement on one of those goals and then we'll work on achieving that goal today.

J: Well I think I need to know things to do . . . what will . . . what is the best way to get David to do what he can do. David you have to be more responsible!

D: It's too hard though, Mom!

J: Well, I think that's something we need to do.

R: I think we can achieve that goal if we have more understanding of the situation . . . what makes David act the way he does . . .

J: First of all, I don't know how we are going to get to that and second of all I don't think that it'll help me know what to do because I'm the one who has to come home and get on him and push him to get it done. I don't think that we are helping him to grow up . . . he's going to have to be a man.

R: I agree with you . . . but I think the way . . . that through understanding what makes him tick, you would know better how to do that.

T: Could you agree on that among the three of you? What about David . . . even though he's eight, he makes a contribution.

R: I find it awfully difficult to put into words that David can understand.

T: Perhaps you and Joan could talk about how you might do that . . . Joan, you mentioned that you deal with David every day relative to his incomplete schoolwork, more frequently apparently than Roy. Maybe you might share some things with Roy that would help him understand a bit better.

J: Well, if you don't . . . I just lost my train of thought.

T: David, could you please switch seats with your dad. If they can sit next to each other, it will be easier for them to talk to each other. Thanks.

J: I've noticed that you just seem reluctant to relate to David about this. You avoid the situation and leave it to me . . . and I don't know. I don't think

I should have to do all this. I don't know whether he thinks we are really serious about all this . . . I think . . . I think none of us want to have to deal with it, not you, not me, not David.

T: It sounds like you are looking for an easier way to do things.

J: You're right. I just get so exasperated any more.

T: Roy?

R: I do leave a lot up to Joan.

T: David, what about you, would you like to be able to do your work easier?

D: Yes. My work . . . it is too hard. Sometimes I can't do it.

T: How about if we pursue that goal . . . how to help David understand how to make his hard work easier, that could incorporate Roy. Your proposal of more understanding and Joan, your proposal of David being more independent.
(Nods of affirmation)

T: I would assume that if David was able to affirm that his work was becoming easier to complete and he began to complete more work in school you all would see that goal as being moved toward.
(Nods of affirmation)

Through directives and indirect information gathering, the therapist confirms further the originally hypothesized A, B, and C. Preliminary strategic change was begun by requesting a physical change in the seating arrangement; to encourage the parents' mutual movement from Roy's non-involvement and Joan's over-involvement to a common middle ground of "teaching" David to debate the very same irrational belief that contributes to Roy's and Joan's (as well as David's) emotional disturbance and the unsuccessful behavioral solution sequences they commonly experience to arrive at and then come to own its rational counterpart.

T: So we're agreed on helping David understand how to make his hard work easier.

J: I just had a thought David. When you say it is too hard, how often do you ask the teacher in the classroom for help? Or do you come to me first?

T: That's a great solution Joan, and maybe we can address that further in a few minutes. Right now, however, we might want to consider more closely how come David thinks that his work is so very hard. You and Roy might want to spend a few minutes first with David finding out why he sees his schoolwork as so very hard.

J: The work that is hard for you that you bring home from school . . . is there a reason that . . . could you help us understand why you see it as too hard to do during class time?

D: I do work in the classroom . . .

J: But David it seems like when you come home . . . out of five assignments, you only have one done.

R: And your teacher writes her little notes saying that David hasn't finished all of his work in school . . . specializing in daydreaming and socializing and playing and not getting all of his work done.

D: I don't know. It's just too hard.

R: I don't think you completely understand what hard means.

T: Roy, an excellent insight. David clearly doesn't seem to understand what hard means. It appears that he's thinking to himself that his classwork is not just difficult, but something much more . . . something unbearable that he has termed "hard."

J: I think that's right on track. He's always saying even relatively simple classwork is too hard. That's the thing that gets me most exasperated because I know it's not too hard for him.

T: What you both appear to be saying is that David is identifying his classwork, which might at times be difficult, but even when not, and thinking about it in a certain way . . . that way being a strong belief "It's too hard!" How realistic do you see his belief?

J: Not realistic at all. I know that some of his classwork isn't easy, but most of it he can do.

T: How helpful would you see that same belief?

J: Not helpful in that he isn't giving himself the chance to do the work then.

T: Roy . . .

R: I agree. It makes a lot of sense.

T: What do you think then might be a more realistic and helpful counterpart to the belief "It's too hard!"? Roy . . .

R: Maybe "It's easy . . ."

T: You might want to consider if that belief is realistic and would it be more helpful because at times the work may actually be difficult or at least somewhat difficult.

R: You've got a point.

J: What about "The work may be hard, but not too hard."

T: Great counterpart to that unrealistic, hurtful belief. How do you think that that belief would be more realistic and helpful for David were he able to learn it?

J: I think that he would see his work as a lot easier and would try harder.

R: I agree.

While Debate has successfully proceeded relative to the parents' debate of their son's irrational belief and confirming a rational counterpart, they have not yet addressed it relative to themselves. The therapist also sensed that Roy, if not both he and Joan, might still be all too ready to move too far in the opposite direction to "It should be easy." The therapist thus moved to Debate simultaneously addressing David but more directly expressing his concerns relative to Roy and Joan's own "It's too hard."

T: That belief . . . "The work may be hard, but not too hard" . . . that as adults looking at David's situation you may not be able to readily empathize with. You may at times be communicating to him the belief that his work should be easy and perhaps it might be helpful to get in touch with what you saw as easy and hard when you were his age. I'm sure that you found some of the work you did hard. I know I did. Can I ask each of you to think back for a second and try to remember yourself being 8 years old and what made your schoolwork hard for you when it was . . . not all of it was, but some of it probably. Could you two talk about your remembrances and maybe that will help you help David better. He just doesn't know.

J: I remember the multiplication tables being hard and I was scared of the teacher.

T: Good remembrance.

D: My teacher might paddle me.

R: I remember how hard it was to concentrate . . . Maybe if David would say to himself "It's hard at first, but I know I can do it." From his record, he should be able to do the schoolwork.

T: Let's stay off of David for a moment. Go back to you own self and your own early experience. You mentioned two things . . . Joan, you were afraid of the teacher when you were 8 years old . . . lots of kids are . . . and Roy, you said that sometimes you had difficulty concentrating. So that's something else that makes schoolwork hard. Are there any other things that you remember when you were 8 years old that made your school work hard for you?

J: I didn't want to ask a question . . . I didn't want to raise my hand and have everybody look at me. I remember that. All the other kids would look at me and I'd get the feeling that I didn't want to raise my hand. I wanted to just sort of hide.

D: Oh Mom, they wouldn't laugh at you.

T: A good point David, but maybe it's more what your mom might have been thinking as opposed to what would have actually happened.

R: I remember every time I was out sick, going back that first day . . . all of the questions and all of the work to make up . . .

T: How about if we look at the things you just mentioned . . . being afraid of the teacher, having difficulty concentrating, just being there and fitting in, and not wanting to ask questions. How hard were they for the two of you then?

J: They were real hard for me.

T: Too hard?

J: At times, yes, that is what I thought.

T: And when you thought that . . .

J: I didn't get my work done either.

T: Roy . . . ever too hard for you then?

R: Yes.

T: And when you thought that . . .

R: I guess I didn't do my work either unless somebody forced me to.

T: It sounds like you both experienced the same unrealistic, hurtful belief as kids that David is now. Do you ever experience that same belief as adults today . . . perhaps even in your dealings with David?

R: That's a sobering thought.

T: Joan . . . you've highlighted your extreme frustration at times. Perhaps "It's too hard" is there in your thinking at those times.

J: You're probably right.

T: Roy . . . you've noted here in our session earlier how you found it just too difficult to continue trying to assist David in understanding what you all were doing here. Was there an "It's too hard" in your thinking as well?

R: Unfortunately I think so.

T: You know. You both are right in assessing working with David as being hard. It certainly is at times. However, is it too hard . . . is it unbearably hard?

J: No, we are his parents and it is our responsibility to help him learn.
(Roy nods in agreement)

T: And so maybe that very same belief you generated earlier of "It's hard, but not too hard" could offer the both of you an understanding of how not only David might make his own work easier but you two might make your teaching David all the easier . . . "It's hard, yes . . .but too hard, no . . . it's clearly not unbearable."

Given that the parents appear more able to own the "family rule" for themselves as well as their son, the process can now shift to Enactment. Time is somewhat limited and so the therapist assumes a more didactic position.

T: Given the apparent belief you all at times share in common of "It's too hard," we want to consider how you Roy and Joan might begin to more consciously keep in the forefront of your own minds, "It's hard, but not too hard" in trying to teach David the same belief. One suggestion I would offer is that you make that more realistic, helpful belief your family motto for the next few weeks. Do you have a family motto?

R: No, I don't think we ever thought about having one before.

T: What do you think would be the conseqences of such a motto?

R: I think it would be easier to keep that thought in the open for us if we looked upon it as our motto.

T: Great. Joan, would you agree?

J: Yes.

T: What might be several ways that you could make use of the motto then. How might you sort of "publicize" it around your home?

J: Well, we could make a poster.

D: We could write it in big letters and put it on the refrigerator where all the notes are put.

T: How else? Perhaps you might begin your dinner meal with a discussion of things you each found hard, but not too hard during that day. Remember, of course, that Roy and Joan, you'll be able to report teaching David each day for a while I'm sure. Are the poster and dinner discussions options you could carry out over the next two weeks?

(All nod in agreement)

T: When might you do the poster?

J: We can do it tomorrow, Saturday.

T: You'll do it as a family, the three of you . . . remember it's your family motto.

(All nod in agreement)

T: One final request . . . after the completing the poster and after each dinner discussion, could you also agree to congratulate each other on using your new family motto? This will be very important to do.

(All nod in agreement)

T: Great! Could I ask that you spend our remaining five minutes just summarizing among yourselves what you've experienced in our demonstration session today and then congratulate yourselves on a job very well done.

The demonstration session concluded with a summary by each of the family members of their thoughts and feelings about the session and then a "Congratulations" à la REFT Feedback. The therapist followed up with the family two weeks after the demonstration session by telephone. They reported preparing the poster and following through on the dinner discussion approximately 10 of the 14 evenings. The therapist spoke with each member individually and asked if he or she thought the goal of the session had been attained using the agreed-upon benchmark identified during the demonstration session. All confirmed (including David) that David was affirming that his work was not all that hard and he was completing significantly more of his classwork in class. The therapist cautioned that relapses were likely and offered the names of a referral source should the "family motto" falter and further therapy efforts be seen as a potentially helpful option.

9

Training and Supervision in REFT

A number of mental health and related disciplines—psychiatry, psychology, social work, nursing, various forms of counseling and the human services—offer direct therapeutic services to troubled families. In many instances, having previously learned therapeutic procedures for working with individuals, practitioners in these disciplines' "family therapy" efforts tend to be gathering a family group together but actually treating individual members within that family context. While these therapists may acknowledge that it is in the context of family life that individual psychopathology develops, they continue to look more singularly upon individual psychopathology as their central concern.

It has been strongly suggested that training and supervision in family therapy calls for a discontinuous learning experience for those clinicians trained in one-to-one psychotherapy (Goldenberg & Goldenberg, 1980). Those seeking to practice REFT should be able to see all behavior, including the manifestation of symptoms in an individual, in its proper context, namely as a consequence of social or interpersonal contributions as well as intrapersonal contributions. The family system *and* the symptomatic person as a part of that system represent the therapeutic unit for achieving change, not just one or the other. In utilizing a view emanating from "cybernetics of cybernetics," the REFT therapist becomes a part of the system, not some outside healer as in many forms of traditional treatment. The passive, neutral, nonjudgmental, uninvolved position advocated so strongly in many forms of traditional individual psychotherapy is best set aside. REFT therapists become involved in families' interpersonal processes (without losing balance or independence), flexibly supporting and nurturing at one point and challenging and confrontive at another. They keep in mind (but not overidentify with) members of different ages, moving swiftly in and out of emotional involvements, while not losing track of family interactions and transaction patterns. Finally, the REFT therapist's focus of treatment is primarily on present transactions, as opposed to a description or recounting of the past. The goal is to facilitate more adaptive problem-solving interactions, not simply interpret or explain them.

In facilitating therapists' adoption of an REFT focus, several areas of tension frequently appear: novice REFT therapists tend to see the identified patient as a victim to be supported as opposed to that recursive complementarity between victimization and active, or at least indirect contribution; novice REFT therapists often become a hub of interactions between and among family members rather than facilitating family members dealing directly with each other; novice REFT therapists often take on the customary role of outside healer as opposed to becoming a participant in the system (being careful to avoid entangling alliances); and finally, novice REFT therapists are at greater risk for being drawn into families' ongoing unsatisfactory problem-solving efforts, by adopting families' irrational beliefs about the system (e.g., jinxed, exploited, powerless) as well as individual family members' irrational beliefs about themselves (e.g., stupid, selfish, unambitious).

How to best train and then supervise the practice of novice REFT therapists will be the concern of this chapter. As a prelude to this discussion, Haley's (1970) comparison of individual-oriented and family-oriented therapies offers introductory considerations. The criteria listed as "family-oriented" in Table 9.1 clearly distinguish those beliefs the REFT therapist would espouse.

SELECTING AN ORIENTATION

Over the years, there have emerged two primary approaches to therapist training and supervision: (1) the psychotherapeutic, and (2) the behavioral approach. Even if the REFT supervisor is not directly familiar with these distinctions, he or she may unintentionally fall into utilizing one or the other since they are universal orientations. Haley (1976) compared these two approaches with regard to several criteria as they apply to the training and supervision of family therapists. In doing so, he offered them as polar opposites, labeling the psychotherapeutic "Orientation A," and the behavioral "Orientation Z."

TABLE 9.1 A Comparison Between Individual-Oriented and Family-Oriented Therapies.

Individual-Oriented	Family-Oriented
1. Family therapy is one of many methods of treatment.	1. Family therapy is a new orientation to viewing human problems.
2. The individual's psychopathology is the focus of study and treatment; the family is seen as a stress factor.	2. The disordered family system needs some family member to express its psychopathology.
3. The identified patient is the victim of family strife.	3. The identified patient contributes to and is an essential part of family strife.
4. The family is a collection of individuals behaving on the basis of past experiences with each other.	4. The present situation is the major causal factor, since current problems must be currently reinforced if they continue to exist.
5. Diagnosis and evaluation of the family problem should precede intervention.	5. Immediate action-oriented intervention takes place at the first session, which is usually a time of family crisis, when the family is ripe for change.
6. The therapist is an observer evaluating the family's problems.	6. The therapist is a part of the context of treatment; his or her active participation affects the family system.
7. The therapist brings out clients' feelings and attitudes toward each other; he or she uses interpretation to show them what they are expressing.	7. The therapist uses fewer interpretations; he or she is interested in enhancing positive aspects of the relationships.
8. The therapist talks to one person at a time; family members talk largely to him rather than to each other.	8. Family members talk to each other, not the therapist; all members are urged to participate.
9. The therapist takes sides in family conflict, supporting one member (for example, a child, a schizophrenic).	9. The therapist avoids being caught up in factional struggles in the family.
10. Family therapy is a technique for gathering additional information about individuals in the family.	10. Individual psychological problems are social problems involving the total ecological system, including the social institutions in which the family is embedded.

From: J. Haley. "Family Therapy," *International Journal of Psychiatry*, 9(1970), 233–242. Copyright (1970) by Baywood Publishing Co., Inc. Reprinted by permission of the publisher and author.

Spontaneous versus Planned Change

Orientation A views the responsibility for therapeutic change as residing with the family members. Within this orientation, it is not the responsibility of the therapist to actively advocate change, but rather to help family members change themselves. The therapist is a reflector or consultant, not an active advocate of change. Normally, the therapist seeks to help family members understand themselves and their situation; what happens then is up to them. Should therapeutic efforts prove unsuccessful, the family members are seen as responsible for the failure, and only partially, if at all, the therapist shares responsibility.

By contrast, Orientation Z views responsiblity for change as residing with the therapist. The therapist is expected to plan a strategy of change to bring about what the family is requesting to achieve. If change does not occur, the therapist is responsible. Projecting responsibility on the family for failure is not allowed.

While these opposite premises are general orientations, they become most evident as the basis for observing operations in actual therapy sessions. In Orientation A, what is to happen between therapist and family members in an upcoming session is unpredictable; it is a happening and cannot be planned since the therapist must wait to see what family members will offer. The therapist is a responder who must wait to comment on, or interpret, what family members initiate. In Orientation Z, the therapist prepares a strategic plan that takes into account what is likely to happen in the upcoming session. The therapist initiates action (e.g., offers a directive for family members to follow, implements a reinforcement program, etc.).

Supervisors adhering to Orientation A act as an advisor or consultant to supervisees. The supervisor is not responsible for the success or failure of therapeutic efforts. If therapy is going poorly, the supervisor may intervene, but generally would still not take responsibility for failure. What happens between supervisee and supervisor is spontaneous and unplanned. The supervisor must wait and see what the supervisee brings; failure is the responsibility of the supervisee. If the supervisor has assisted the supervisee understand him or herself and the dynamics of the case, the supervisor has done a credible job.

Supervisors adhering to Orientation Z take responsibility for what happens with a case and actively plan with the supervisee what is likely to happen. Where "live" supervision is an option, the supervisor views the supervisee's work through a one-way mirror. The supervisor telephones the supervisee during the session and offers guidance, if necessary, or requests the supervisee come out of the session to discuss what is occurring. In this arrangement, if change is not taking place, the supervisor takes responsibility. Not only is it the supervisor's job to protect family members from the supervisees' mistakes, he or she also aids the supervisee in difficulty. If family members are provoking a supervisee and so blocking therapeutic movement, the supervisor's job is to find a way to help the supervisee solve that problem. Just as the supervisee seeks to actively advocate family members' changing if their life circumstances are unsatisfactory, so too the supervisor seeks to find a way to actively advocate supervisee change if the supervisee's work with a family is going poorly.

A Growth versus a Problem Orientation

Orientation A posits the primary goal of family therapy to be the expansion of the life of family members. Orientation Z posits that primary goal as the solution of specific problems. Orientation A is based on the premise that the goal of therapy is to assist family members to develop themselves and so the therapist's task is essentially an educational one. The therapist focuses on enriching family members' lives. If a family presents a child as a problem because he or she sets fires, the therapists' goal is the development of the child or family. The fire setting is thus "only a symptom." By contrast, Orientation Z views the therapist as a problem solver. The therapist clarifies and assists family members address the specific problems they present for therapy. If a child is presented as a problem because he sets fires, the therapist's goal is to actively arrange that the child no longer set fires. In the process of solving the fire setting, organizational changes may be made that allow the child and parents to grow and develop, but the focus is on the symptom.

These two orientations contribute to quite different therapeutic procedures. Orientation A tends to leave the details of the presenting symptoms unexamined and to focus instead on the general background of family members. Directives are not utilized to facilitate change. Instead, procedures are interpretive or experiential. Therapists often attempt to persuade family members that what they want is something other than the complaint they offer. For example, parents who present a child as the problem may be influenced to see their marriage as the "real" problem. Or, the therapist may describe a child as "scapegoated," seeing the primary therapeutic task as pointing out other children who are problems, to get the problem child out of the scapegoat role. In contrast, Orientation Z accepts what family members offer as the problem and focus on that. If a symptom is offered, the therapist seeks to engineer change through the symptom. If a child is offered as the problem, the therapist accepts the description and only later possibly shifts to other children or marital issues.

Training and supervision within Orientation A is conceived of as providing supervisees with a rich philosophical life and facilitating individual growth. The trend is toward assisting the supervisee to grow and develop. Instead of becoming competent in specific therapeutic skills, the supervisee is encouraged to enter therapy him or herself so as to discover from personal experience what the human mind is all about. It is assumed that the supervision and personal therapy will contribute to a mature, developed individual and also an expert therapist. At the other end of the continuum, Orientation Z assumes that a supervisee grows with success in his or her work and thus the primary training and supervisory task is to facilitate the supervisee in doing successful therapy. The focus is on assisting supervisees to solve the problems they confront in working with families, not helping them enrich their personal lives. For example, if a supervisee has difficulty dealing with an authority figure in the family during therapy, Orientation Z would advocate training the supervisee to better deal with family authority figures. Orientation A, by contrast, would advocate encouraging the supervisee to understand his or her personal feelings about family authority figures and to resolve that personal problem.

As seen in another manner, Orientation A proposes that family members should welcome therapy because it is good for people and will make them part of a special elite who have had a unique experience. Orientation Z posits therapy as an experience for family members in distress wishing to get back to normal.

Understanding versus Action as a Contributor to Change

Orientation A assumes that family members should be more self-aware. The premise espoused is that if family members understand what they are doing, and why, they won't do it anymore. Therefore, it is the therapist's task to help family members understand themselves both cognitively and experientially. Lifting of repression by making conscious the unconscious within a transference framework, or making interpretations about communication to help family members understand how they are dealing with one another are representative of the type of therapeutic approach taken. Orientation A also sometimes includes the idea that if family members express their emotions, they will change, and so the honest and open expression of "real" feelings is emphasized. Within this orientation, supervision typically focuses on individual dynamics including the past history that led up to the presenting problem, and/or family interaction process and dynamics. Supervision involves discussion of the ways family members interact in both verbal and nonverbal ways. Little or no emphasis is given as to what to do to bring about change.

Within Orientation Z, it is assumed that neither understanding nor the expression of emotion causes change. Therefore, therapy's primary focus is not interpretation or uncovering. Instead, the therapist plans a strategy and devises directives requiring new behaviors. These directives may be strategic behavior change programs for an individual family member or the entire family. Supervision involves little discussion of dynamics and a great deal of discussion of what to do in the therapy and how to do it. Orientation Z assumes that symptoms cannot be resolved or a problem solved by merely talking about them. Therefore, both therapy and supervision emphasize bringing the problem into the therapy session. If a child has temper tantrums and bangs her head, having only a discussion about this behavior is not likely to lead to change. What is required is action—the head banging should happen in the therapy session. If a couple has a problem of fighting, they should fight in the therapy session. Of course, some problems cannot be brought into the session, but those that can should be put into action and dealt with in the session. Likewise, training and supervision within Orientation A reflect the assumption that supervisees learn by understanding themselves and therefore consist of conversation about the supervisee's conduct with a case. Orientation Z assumes that the problems of the supervisee best appear in action before the supervisor.

Because of the emphasis on self-awareness and individual experience, therapists within Orientation A often bring families together in family group therapy. By bringing several families together, it is assumed that members will learn from each other; thus, understanding their own families differently, will change. In Orientation Z, it is the behavior within the natural group, the family itself, that must change. The therapist tries to change repeating sequences involving these several persons who are habitually together. A husband may understand how other husbands relate to their wives in a family group therapy setting, but that does not mean he will change his relationship with his wife. To change in relation to his wife, he should be in therapy that focuses the interactions he and his wife have, not those of couples around them.

Within Orientation A, it is occasionally assumed that if therapists understand their own personal involvement with family members, they will be competent therapists. The supervisor's talk is intended to increase supervisees' awareness of their biases and to change their way of thinking. Supervisees are also urged to understand their involvement with their own family as well in order to become good therapists. Given these assumptions, supervisees are urged to enter personal therapy or to have encounter experiences in groups. One premise of this persuasion is the idea that since family members are expected to confess all about themselves, the supervisee is also expected to have experienced confessing all. Within Orientation A, supervisees may also be expected to go through simulated family exercises revealing their ideas and feelings about their own families. They may be assigned the task of contacting relatives to activate their extended family network to help understand their involvement in their wider family.

Orientation Z does not assume that therapists will be more effective if they understand themselves or freely express their emotions. Instead, it assumes that therapists will improve as therapists only by doing therapy under supervision and improving their skills. Instead of helping supervisees understand personal feelings in a case, the supervisor will offer active ways to resolve the difficulties in the case. The supervisor teaches supervisees ways to use themselves to bring about change. It is assumed that supervisees will change with action, not reflection about themselves. Just as the families treated by this approach are not expected to confess all, neither are supervisees in training and supervision. Within Orientation Z, group exercises involving supervisees having experiences together or sculpting their own family concerns would not be done, since these would detract supervisees from the primary task, that being family change.

Self-Report versus Observation

Therapists within Orientation A tend to consider the ideas and fantasies of family members more relevant to therapy than family members' actual life circumstances. Therefore, they often feel it unnecessary to observe how family members interact; self-report is accepted as adequate data. In sessions with whole families present, action among family members is not encouraged. Instead, each family member is asked about what happens in the family and reports about it to the therapist.

Orientation Z casts grave doubt about the reliability of self-report. The predominant concern is what is actually happening rather than family members' ideas about what is happening. Orientation Z holds that what persons say about their family or marriage and what might be observed can be markedly different. When whole families are seen, members are asked to deal with each other so that the therapist can see how they do that rather than listen to them describe how they do that.

Within Orientation A, the supervisor tends to accept the self-reports of supervisees. Supervisees make notes and take them to the supervisor who tries to guess what might have happened from that self-report. Lacking any other observable data, the supervisor naturally tends to discuss supervisees' ideas and fantasies about cases. In Orientation Z, the supervisor observes supervisees in action with families either live, through a one-way mirror, or on videotape or audiotape. The supervisor does not believe supervisees can accurately report what happened, just as family members cannot accurately report what happens in their family. The supervisor in Orientation Z wants the action in front of him or her so it can be observed, recognizing that what supervisees say about a session and what could be observed in a session may be quite different. Training and supervision are concerned with what really happens in therapy sessions, and therefore predominantly with therapy skills, not the content of supervisees' fantasies.

In summary then, it can be seen that Orientation A, the psychotherapeutic approach to training and supervision, is similar to that approach to therapy; supervisors provide a therapeutic relationship to supervisees in which the dynamics of therapy efforts can be explored and constructively altered. Together they examine the interaction or interpersonal dynamics between the supervisee and family members, and between and among family members. The purpose of such examination is to uncover dynamic patterns which might inhibit therapy progress. If and when these patterns are discovered, the supervisor employs psychotherapy procedures to assist supervisees change troublesome dynamics. Psychotherapeutic supervision does not restrict itself to the dynamics in therapy, but also attends to dynamics within supervision as well. Supervisees' emotions toward the supervisor may be investigated, and supervisors themselves may share and discuss their own dynamics. The overriding objective of psychotherapeutic training and supervision is to teach supervisees to be a monitor of their own dynamics and to use these dynamics therapeutically.

Orientation Z, the behavioral approach to training and supervision, contrasts the psychotherapeutic approach in its focus on action and skills as opposed to dynamics. The purpose of behavioral supervision is to assist supervisees to eliminate inappropriate social behaviors and ineffective therapy procedures from their therapeutic repertoire, and to promote the development and practice of effective therapy procedures.

Both the behavioral and psychotherapeutic approaches to training and supervision are widely accepted and practiced and each has received empirical support (Boyd, 1978). The REFT supervisor is thus left with a choice—which approach will be the better for fostering the competent practice of REFT? Advocated throughout this book has been the higher order view of "cybernetics of cybernetics." Rather than proposing the psychotherapeutic and behavioral approaches to training and supervision as related through a logic of negation (e.g., A/not Z, or Z/not A), cybernetics of cybernetics posits a logic of complementarity evidenced in a "poly-ocular view." This view is taken herein and proposes that fusing the psychotherapeutic and behavioral distinctions will produce a bonus, a higher order view. Relative to training and supervision from a Rational–Emotive position, this higher order view has been termed *A Psychobehavioral Approach* (Grieger & Boyd, 1980).

THE TASKS OF REFT SUPERVISION

Supervision has commonly been conceptualized as a process wherein a supervisor monitors a supervisee's actual practice of therapy while facilitating the effective employment of skills and/or personal understandings learned during training. The implication is that training should precede supervision. While this is certainly an ideal worthy of pursuit, it tends to often be an exception as opposed to the rule. Training does not always precede supervision and so supervisees do not always have a fully developed repertoire of personal understandings and/or therapeutic skills and understandings. This is particularly true in the supervision of REFT. While many supervisees may have an extensive background in *individual-oriented* RET, they lack the systemic skills and understandings essential to the *family-oriented* practice of REFT. In expected practice then, the REFT supervisor had better be prepared to deal with supervisees having a wide range of training backgrounds and skills and understandings proficiencies. Thus, REFT training herein is seen as a holon within the larger supervision suprasystem at times, as well as an independent endeavor at other times. This chapter focuses on the former although the present discussion applies equally to the latter as well.

As REFT posits a stance of flexibility—a willingness to seek out alternative beliefs and solutions—so too REFT supervision reflects an "openness to new experience." Its primary focus for doing so is the position that supervision consists of *multiple tasks*. Three major tasks generally comprise the supervision process: (1) teaching procedures; (2) facilitating mastery of shifting presuppositions; and (3) facilitating movement beyond barriers to results (O'Hanlon & Wilk, 1987).

Providing Training and Guidance in Specific Procedures

Supervision is used to teach novice therapists the essential clinical procedures involved in REFT, or to pass along more advanced procedures to intermediate and experienced practitioners. Before the widespread use of *direct observation* (co- and team therapy, one-way mirrors, and video- and audiotaping), therapists were supervised in the practice of therapy through *description* (general case discussion, anecdotal reporting, or personal experience as clients). Both of these teaching contexts have their value, but each is of limited use in specifying the actions that make up clinical practice. The questions in most beginning therapists' minds, "What do I say?" and "What do I do? (questions by no means confined only to novice therapists), are not readily or most usefully answered by either of these two means individually.

REFT supervision emphasizes *both description and observation* as core elements of supervision. Observational supervisory methods—videotape, audiotape, one-way mirror, team therapy, and cotherapy—are employed by supervisors either to instruct supervisees by modeling examples of specific procedures, or to offer supervisees corrective comments on their overt actions. The descriptive component accompanies the observational component and offers information not readily available to overt observation (i.e., thoughts, feelings, images). Supervisors' request that supervisees present cases for supervision in both observational and descriptive terms enables more comprehensive supervisory learning to occur.

REFT supervision employs experiential learning, didactic instruction, modeling/observational learning, and skill practice and shaping. These modalities are equally applicable for facilitating training and guidance in specific procedures within the aforementioned supervisory context.

Facilitating Mastery of Shifting Presuppositions

Identifying and specifying the underlying presuppositions of REFT as a particular approach to the practice of family therapy is of critical value in avoiding many of the typical struggles of supervision. Often supervisor and supervisee find themselves playing "dualing paradigms," each operating from a different set of assumptions and guidelines for results and not recognizing the area of disagreement. It is sometimes as if supervisees learning a new approach to working with families have to "get it" by osmosis, rather than through explicit guidance and understanding.

The emphasis in REFT supervision is on being able to specify those presuppositions essential to the effective practice of REFT. This makes it easier for the supervisor and supervisee to highlight important points and to ferret out presuppositions that may be in conflict with REFT. In this way, supervisees can be aided in mastering the necessary shift from one set of presuppositions to another (i.e., REFT), as well as mastering the very process of shifting presuppositions more easily.

Facilitating Movement Beyond Barriers to Results

The third main task of REFT supervision is assisting supervisees who are "stuck" get "unstuck." As with client families, supervisees who aren't getting the results they desire should best consider doing something different or differently, or stop doing something they are currently doing. In essence, most all that has been described throughout this book under the rubric of therapy is applicable to the supervision setting, with the supervisee–family/client "system" as the "client" in this case. The beginning—"What brings you here?"—is the same as in therapy, and the ABCDEF is proceeded through in like manner, with the supervisor eliciting the supervisee's experience of each component therein (via both observational and descriptive input).

If REFT supervisors were closely observed as they interact with supervisees, they would be seen moving from one of these tasks to another. They would stress the essential elements of REFT as the context for supervisees' work with families. Should supervisees encounter problems with therapeutic procedures, the supervisors would do some skills teaching, perhaps by modeling and skills practice within the supervisory session, or in the case of co- or team therapy, in the actual therapy session. If supervisees encountered emotional concerns which disrupted their work, supervisors would offer REFT therapeutic assistance. To summarize, REFT supervision is not a rigid and narrow process but a rather broad one having multiple tasks among which the supervisor is continually moving.

REFT SUPERVISION:
A PSYCHOBEHAVIORAL APPROACH

REFT's psychobehavioral approach to supervision consists of remaining alert to three kinds of supervisee concerns, and then addressing these concerns by teaching therapeutic procedures, delineating REFT presuppositions, and/or REFT therapeutic intervention. The three most common supervisee concerns experienced in REFT supervision include: (1) emotional concerns, (2) procedural concerns, and (3) emotional/procedural concerns (Grieger & Boyd, 1980). The emotional concerns of supervisees come from several sources—their private lives, therapy-based upsets, and supervision-based upsets. Private life concerns are such things as relationship breakup, financial difficulties, or the illness or death of an intimate. Illustrations of emotional concerns relative to therapy include anger toward certain family members, feelings of incompetence in the role of therapist, or frustration over imperfect therapy performance. Supervision-based emotional concerns include demands for a supervisor's approval, catastrophizing over disapproval, discomfort anxiety relative to participating in co- or team therapy, etc.

Supervisees' procedural concerns consist of skill deficits and/or performance difficulties. When supervisees have minor skill deficits, the supervisor institutes remedial training; major deficits indicate the supervisee is unprepared for actual practice with families until more extensive training objectives are agreed upon and attained. Performance difficulties, in contrast to skill deficits, are to be expected. Almost all supervisees require refinement of their therapeutic procedures, something that comes only through continuing experience with families in session and supervisory critique. Though supervisees may be clear about REFT presuppositions and have the essential skills in their therapeutic repertoire, under the pressures of actual family therapy, they may sometimes be at a loss as to *when* and *how* to use them.

Finally, supervisees can present emotional/procedural concerns. These combine the two prior concerns and are particularly difficult for supervisors because the supervisee is emotionally upset *and* performing inadequately. In these dual concerns in particular, the benefits of REFT supervision via a psychobehavioral approach is best evidenced because neither the psychotherapeutic nor the behavioral would necessarily prove sufficient alone for effective and efficient problem resolution.

Grieger and Boyd (1980) expounded upon the psychobehavioral approach to supervision by offering specific recommendations relative to the concerns presented by supervisees. The following discussion follows their basic recommendations while simultaneously going beyond them in their application within REFT supervision.

Supervisees' Emotional Concerns

Emotional concerns from supervisees' private lives will not be addressed here because they are the same as those for clients as touched upon throughout earlier chapters of this book. It would be remiss, however, not to note supervisors' responsibility to discourage seriously distressed supervisees from REFT practice. The disturbed supervisee can be referred to an REFT therapist and resume supervised practice when the emotional problem is resolved.

Emotional concerns emanating from therapy and supervision deserve special mention, for they are almost inevitable. Common among the concerns most frequently presented are:

Impatience: Supervisees sometimes demand that they quickly and easily become proficient in REFT practice. They become frustrated at the slowness of their progress. The more frustrated they become, the more they inhibit their progress.

Perfectionism: Some supervisees set unrealistically high standards for their therapy and/or supervision performance and then fear that they will err too often. Upon making inevitable mistakes, they compound the mistakes by self-damning and catastrophizing.

Anger: Supervisees at times have difficulty making constructive use of supervisory feedback. These supervisees usually demand total approval from the supervisor and when they don't get it, become enraged.

Dependency: Supervisees who constantly seek the supervisor's advice for fear of making mistakes tend to see themselves as weak and incapable. They are dependent to the extreme of being unable to learn by their own initiative. Their emotional dependency significantly inhibits the supervisory process.

Upset with client family members: There are many kinds of emotional upsets supervisees can have with family members they are seeing in therapy. They can be angry at them, feel exaggerated sympathy for them, be frustrated with regard to their lack of immediate improvement, etc. These emotional concerns are contributed to by supervisees' over-personalizing therapeutic relationships with families, as well as imbuing the interaction with relationship concerns emanating from their own family of origin.

The REFT supervisor deals directly with supervisees' emotional concerns of this type, practicing REFT. Supervision, however, does not become only therapy; excursions into therapy are relatively brief. Even when emotional concerns require a majority of a supervision session, at least one-fourth is best reserved for procedural concerns and/or enhancement.

Supervisees' Procedural Concerns

Addressing supervisees' procedural concerns begins by asking, "Where in the REFT process has the supervisee's work with this family progressed?" Answering this question will help to orient the supervisor and supervisee, suggesting which therapy procedures and objectives are timely. If the supervisee and family members have reached the point of strategic intervention strategies (i.e., debate, enactment, feedback) but performed poorly and missed objectives at earlier points in the therapy (e.g., assessing family frames of reference relative to A, B, C), it is best to backtrack. Illustratively, difficulties in debate may indicate that family members had not been afforded Rational-Emotive insight during the assessment of A, B, C. A quick check by supervisee and supervisor into prior sessions with the family will offer support, and if insight was not accomplished, the supervisee can be assisted in returning to this objective with an alternative plan in mind.

Backtracking is not necessarily a sign of ineffective REFT; experienced therapists have learned to monitor the therapy process and family members' reactions, recognizing when objectives might have been missed in earlier sessions. It is thus experientially important for supervisees to continually access their locus in the process, and to review past sessions for possible oversights. Common performance concerns frequently found in REFT supervision include the following:

Conceptual confusions: It is rare when family members present a coherent, organized presentation of their concerns. They frequently complain of a plethora of problems. This confusion requires supervisees to facilitate order in the midst of chaos; prioritizing concerns, identifying ABC sequences, particularly tuning into family members' irrational beliefs. The potential for confusion is great and, without a thorough knowledge of REFT theory and procedures, errors are likely. The supervision direction is, of course, to generate greater familiarity with REFT.

The big picture trap: This is a performance concern to unsophisticated and less confident supervisees. These supervisees seek to obtain a total picture of the family's past, present, and future before moving to strategic change processes. Unsophisticated supervisees know no better while those less confident believe they need to do this. These supervisees lack the understanding that obtaining a perfectly complete picture is neither necessary nor advisable. Supervision entails facilitating a greater understanding of the ABC conceptualization and those irrational beliefs contributing to major emotional disturbance and unsuccessful problem-solving. When supervisees recognize that two main ideas significantly contribute to guilt, for example: 1. "I did something bad," and 2. "because I did that bad thing, I am bad" they will quickly see these themes in a family member's current thinking when presented with a guilt concern without having to excessively assess "the big picture."

Assuming too much: Because the ABC conceptualization is relatively simple, and because the major irrational beliefs that contribute to families' problems are fairly apparent to one familiar with REFT, many supervisees incorrectly assume that family members are accurately aware of their irrational ideas, confirm that they contribute to disturbing emotions and unsatisfactory behavioral solution sequences, etc. Believing this, the supervisee prematurely moves forward into strategic change processes resulting in confusion and frustration for all. Supervision in such instances engenders greater attentiveness to discrepancies in family members' verbal and nonverbal reports and interactions. For instance, family members may report demands for mutual expressions of affection, yet because of more significant irrational beliefs about their own individual lack of worth, be unwilling to accept those expressions of affection. Supervisees in such circumstances benefit from expressing the value of not assuming insight before insight occurs.

Lecturing/telling: Even though REFT advocates an active, directive therapist stance, a common supervisee procedural concern is doing *too much* telling or lecturing. This contributes to families who do very little work in therapy, being ineffective, passive listeners. Lecturing/ telling tends to lead to very superficial solutions which families are ill-prepared to implement. Supervision herein facilitates the understanding that family members are less likely to relate to insights when primarily told about them as opposed to having the opportunity to rigorously think and act them through. The primary emphasis for supervision relative to the procedural concern: Do only as much lecturing/telling as necessary to facilitate families to do their own thinking and acting.

Philosophizing: A procedural concern similar to lecturing/telling through which supervisees and family members with them can make ill use of time together is philosophizing. As Harris (1977) noted, supervisees can readily get caught up in the philosophical under-pinnings of REFT and slip into abstract (though possibly quite brilliant) monolgues. Such excess verbiage contributes to family members externalizing core concerns and postponing their own Debate. Supervision here focuses on how the supervisee can facilitate family members' struggling to debate their own irrational and rational ideas, rather than listen to the supervisee's philosophical monologues about those ideas.

Unevocative questioning: Like lecturing/telling, philosophizing, and other types of longwinded verbal expositions, unevocative questioning (i.e., asking questions which do not promote family members' own thought) tend not to promote Debate and with it, more rational thinking. Difficult to immediately recognize unevocative questioning requires close inspection to spot. At first glance, a supervisee might appear to be doing well at questioning, but observation of family members' responses or lack thereof shows that the questions are washouts. Harris (1977) identified several ways this procedural concern is evidenced, one being rhetorical questions for which no response is necessary. A rapid-fire string of questions is another, for family members either have no opportunity to answer or can answer the least challenging question posed them. An even more inefficient form of questioning is those questions which the supervisee answers. Supervision would emphasize procedural training focusing on evocative, open-ended, confrontive questions. For example: "What might you be thinking when you experience those upsetting feelings?" instead of "Are you feeling upset again?"

Failure to emphasize gains: As family members implement a new solution at E following effective debate at D, it is important that they are able to self-affirm at F if successful. Family members, however, are sometimes poor evaluators of their own progress; supervisees who don't underscore even relatively small gains may find family members beginning to think therapeutic efforts are to no avail.

Blindly accepting gains: Another procedural concern, somewhat opposite to the previous one, is assuming that family members are applying in their daily interactions what they have done in therapy sessions. Two issues are involved here. One is whether or not family members are making use of their rational thinking, and a second is whether or not they apply these rational thoughts across various life situations as opposed to just one. Supervisees often get seduced into thinking family members are both applying and generalizing rational ideas in their daily lives because they can articulate rational conversations with the supervisee. Supervision here would focus on the importance of supervisees' facilitating family members' enactment in session of representative isomorphs from their daily lives. It is also important to enact with family members in session representative circumstances wherein they might extend rational thinking into divergent areas of their daily living.

Supervisees' Emotional/Procedural Concerns

In the ongoing course of REFT supervision, attention to identified emotional concerns or identified procedural concerns is given as each might be highlighted by supervisor and supervisee. The supervision alternates between REFT and teaching procedures and presuppositions. When an emotional/procedural concern is expressed, the emotional aspect is addressed first. This is because REFT, as emphasized in earlier chapters, posits that emotional disturbance tends to significantly disrupt behavioral performance. By resolving supervisees' emotional concerns, procedural performance often improves, although not always. In these latter cases, teaching procedures and/or presuppositions would follow.

One common illustration of an emotional/procedural concern is supervisees' failure to accept family members' fallibility. A philosophic cornerstone of REFT is that all people are fallible and will regularly make mistakes (sometimes many) in the course of their lives. Supervisees occasionally fall prey to demanding perfection from family members. This may emanate from their own perfectionistic beliefs about their self-worth being wedded to their success with families; other times it is contributed to by their failure to recognize that family members will be incompletely and imperfectly rational in therapy, just as they will be imperfect in other areas of their lives. Regardless, supervisees who demand perfection will tend to keep hammering (i.e., lecturing/telling, unevocative questioning, etc.) away at them to do more and more, to get better and better. Supervision here would engage an ABCDEF encounter between supervisor and supervisee which would also include teaching different procedures to take the place of those "hammering" actions.

AN REFT SUPERVISION SESSION

The typical REFT supervision session has the same efficiency as an REFT therapy session. The process is not rushed, but proceeds as calmly and surely as possible in following a basic set of presuppositions and procedures. Grieger and Boyd's (1980) outline of RET supervision has been the model generally adopted for REFT supervision.

1. Supervision takes place on a regularly scheduled basis. If supervision is not "live," supervisees record their REFT sessions on audio and/or videotape and bring these taped sessions to supervision.

2. Supervisees review their tapes prior to the supervision session, selecting portions of the tapes to present in supervision. Occasionally, the supervisor will preview a tape prior to the supervision session and select excerpts to highlight in an upcoming session with a supervisee.

3. A brief background and/or progress report is prepared by the supervisee to accompany taped session excerpts and/or in preparation for "live" supervision. This report also includes the supervisee's goals for this specific supervision session. By reading this at the beginning of the session, the supervisor is oriented to the family, or if already familiar with the family, to their recent efforts with the supervisee. The supervisor is also able to become oriented to the supervisee's desired goals for the session. Brief report writing such as this reduces information gathering time during the session and also facilitates supervisees in consolidating their agenda for both their client families and supervision.

4. Supervision sessions normally begin by confirming the supervisee's goals for the session followed by a review of any outside-of-supervision tasks agreed to be completed in the interim since the last supervision session ("homework").

5. The focus then shifts to the supervisee's case(s) to be presented (or observed, if "live" supervision).

6. The psychobehavioral approach is the model for reviewing therapy tapes and critiquing "live" supervision. Questions addressed include:

- At what point in the process is this session?
- What are the primary tasks at this particular point and how are they being facilitated; what procedures are best here?

- What emotional actions and reactions are present; are they tending to be facilitative?

7. When procedural deficiencies or performance difficulties are observed, procedural training is employed; typically an enactment occurs within the session and a homework task is agreed upon that continues procedural training outside of the supervision session.

8. A particular procedural deficiency, performance difficulty, or question relative to shifting presuppositions may receive continuing attention in supervison even if not immediately germane to a specific family being seen by the supervisee. In-session enactments and homework tasks would represent an integral part of this continuing attention until sufficient proficiency is acknowledged as having been attained.

9. When supervisee emotional concerns are encountered, the supervision session shifts more toward a therapy session, with supervisor as REFT therapist.

10. The REFT supervision session closes with a summarization of its content and process by supervisor and supervisee. Homework tasks constructed during the session are confirmed and/or homework tasks are constucted and agreed to emanating from the overall session and session summarization by which emotional, procedural, and/or emotional/procedural concerns can be addressed during the interim before the next supervision session.

The following verbatim transcription of a recorded REFT supervision session illustrates this outlined process.

Supervisee: Susan (S)
Supervisor: C. Huber (CH)

S: My goal for today's supervision . . . today what I'd like to do is take the case I've brought in a videotape of and critique my understanding of how I moved with this couple using the ABCs as we addressed last session. My homework was to seek to be more specific in getting to the ABCs with a couple or family and I've brought in an excerpt from my session with Karen and Mike to illustrate my attempting to do so.

CH: Sounds great. Can you offer me some background as a prelude to viewing the tape?

S: This is a couple who has been in therapy with a lot of different therapists. They've been married 11 years and have 3 children, 10, 8, and 7. She is committed to working through their problems in therapy and he thinks therapy is a large waste of time and only comes to placate her. There's been a lot of fighting, in fact, they seem to fight about everything. The most pressing issue at the moment seems to be her being highly critical of his style of interacting with their son which she perceives to be devastating to the boy. She sees him as hypercritical . . . they both claim to have completely different ideas about childrearing. They both claim to come out of very different families of origin and instead of accommodating to each other when they married, they just continued along what they call "parallel paths." In essence, if I were to draw the relationship they represent two circles with no overlap. They see themselves as never having really come together and worked through who's supposed to do what in the relationship. The intrusion of children made it even more awkward and difficult. That is the point at which they originally sought therapy almost 8 years ago. Since, they've been going off and on with a multitude of different professionals.

CH: Let's look specifically at how you were able to be clear with the ABCs. Can you give me an overview of that before we view the tape?

S: They identified three priority goals. To improve communication between them, to make their expectations of each other more realistic; and to determine what areas of commonality they might build on to accommodate more readily. It was very difficult to get them to prioritize because they fight about everything. I mean everything. Hello is an argument.

CH: Were you able to identify benchmarks . . . how they'll know when they are communicating better? I assume you began with their first prioritized goal.

S: Yes. They identified two benchmarks. The first is that they will stop attacking when they deliver messages to each other. The second is that they will be able to better recognize that the other is hearing and acknowledging what they're saying. Those were their two benchmarks.

CH: Great. What about C? What solutions have they attempted and how do they feel repeating the same unsuccessful solutions?

S: The main solution they repeat unsuccessfully is to keep trying to convince. She keeps trying to convince him of how critical he is and how wrong he is. He argues right back in trying to convince her that she's the one who's wrong. They both feel discounted, angry, and very frustrated.

CH: What about the B? What were you all able to distill as their dominant rule?

S: The rule is "I must win; I must be right; he or she has got to act differently."

CH: You seem to have gotten the A, the C, and the B well specified.

S: I'd like to view the videotape now. We got that far in the session but there is another part of this that I find particularly disturbing. I posed the rule of "I must win or be right or be in control." Then I asked them in what ways they might modify the rule. They found it somewhat gamey and they would break into big smiles or laughs about what was going on. Like all that we were doing was a big joke.

CH: Let's go ahead and view the excerpt you've identified.

(Excerpt of videotape is viewed)

CH: What was going on there for you when you found them being gamey and laughing?

S: Something was wrong . . . I sort of felt caught. I wanted them to stop it and be serious about what we were doing.

CH: OK. let's look at that and let's put the interaction into an ABC framing for you. For you, what was the A?

S: Them snickering.

CH: And what would you have liked to see happen instead . . . what would be your goal?

S: I would want them to be serious about the therapy.

CH: What about a benchmark or two? How would you be able to identify for yourself that they were being serious about the therapy?

S: For one thing, they wouldn't be snickering. They would stay on task.

CH: So, if they snickered less and stayed on task more, you would see your goal of them being more serious about the therapy as having been attained?

S: Right.

CH: When they were snickering, how were you feeling?

S: On the outside, excluded.

CH: It looked like you were experiencing some significant irritation as well.

S: Yes, I was becoming pretty angry.

CH: Although we just viewed it on the tape, could you recap what your response was to their snickering. How did you try to get them to be more serious?

S: I asked them "What's going on here?"

CH: Sort of angrily it appeared.

S: You're right. I was feeling my level of arousal rising.

CH: You asked, perhaps challenged them with that response. How did you see that as having worked? Did that solution work satisfactorily?

S: No, because they continued snickering even more after I asked it.

CH: And so given that that solution wasn't satisfactory, they're still snickering, and you're feeling even more angry, what possibly might be the belief you were thinking at that moment?

S: The belief I had was that they think this is a joke.

CH: They think this is a joke and . . . ?

S: And they really don't want to work at this.

CH: They really don't want to work at this and they . . . ?

S: And they must!

CH: How helpful is that belief if it leaves you angry and leads to a solution that apparently only intensified their snickering?

S: Not very helpful. I see where you're going. It wasn't very realistic either in that I can't demand that they be more serious.

CH: For sure. If that belief's not helpful for you and also rather unrealistic, the next question becomes what might be a more realistic and helpful belief that communicates "stay the same but change" while introducing some meaningful new information?

S: Maybe I want, not demand, them to be more serious and maybe I should also reexamine what that snickering means and/or if it even is that disruptive to the process.

CH: Great. Let's go back now and look at the same videotape excerpt and then consider how you might have acted differently given your altered belief.

(Excerpt of videotape is re-viewed)

CH: Think about the rule they're applying right then and there with you.

S: We must win. We must be in control.

CH: And how foolish it is, Susan, to even think you could be right and we wrong. How can you tell us something more than we already know? Can you see how all three of you were operating under the same core demandingness?

S: I see that now, particularly in reviewing the tape.

CH: How might you facilitate their debating that rule? You might want to stress even more the demanding aspect of their belief, and maybe your own as well. Perhaps "I must be right; he or she must act differently 100% of the time!"

S: I think I tried to do just that later in this session. As we just critiqued, I found myself getting angry and I finally confronted them with what the snickering was all about. We ended up addressing a different solution. I don't think I made much headway with dispute of their rule at all.

CH: It sounds like you might have moved ahead a bit soon to Enactment; that being considering a different solution . . . but you'd want to do that only after a more rational rule has been arrived at.

S: It's becoming more clear to me now.

CH: Good. You might want to consider how you can stay with Debate before moving to Enactment until you and they are clearer about the altered rule prior to moving to an alternative solution.

S: And stay with it, meaning?

CH: Meaning what's their more rational belief, the more rational alternative to "I must be right; he or she must act differently 100% of the time!"

S: I see. So it would have been a better move to stick with the belief at D.

CH: If we're looking at their mutual irrational belief as being the key contributor; the A, B, and C have been identified very well. Moving to Debate seeks to answer the questions of "How realistic?" and "How helpful?" is that irrational belief?

S: This I would see them as snickering about.

CH: That's where you might want to Debate your own irrational belief that they must be serious 100% of the session. What might be a more rational belief, one that is more realistic and helpful for you?

S: That I want them to be serious, but that they won't likely be all the time. I need to expect their snickering at times.

CH: Great. With that firmly in mind, how might you communicate to them
     "stay the same, change," and offer them meaningful new information?
S: What I might say is something like this, "It's important to you and you each
     want to be right but do you absolutely have to be right; and is it even possible
     to be right 100% of the time?" Then we would look at another solution.
CH: Try and stay with the belief longer as opposed to moving to another solution
     so quickly.
S: I don't want to come up with another solution; just a more rational belief.
CH: For right now.
S: I might not have done that enough this last session. I mean they acknowl-
     edged that they commonly held the irrational belief.
CH: That's where you wanted to go; you were right on track but just confirming
     the hurtful effects of the irrational belief is insufficient. There also needs to
     be a more rational rule to take its place and offer direction to an alternative
     solution.
S: Well, we did come up with the alternative that there could be more negotia-
     tion, but that is more of a behavioral solution.
CH: You want to facilitate during Debate a confirmation that their present rule
     is not helping them by questioning how realistic, how sensible, how helpful
     it is for them to maintain it. Then determine what might be a more realistic,
     more sensible, more helpful belief. You're actually posing two sides and
     proposing that they can think to themselves "I must be right; he or she
     must act differently 100% of the time" versus "I want to be right; however,
     that rightness can be shared 50/50." Which of those rules will be more realis-
     tic, sensible, helpful and why and how?
S: I see.
CH: Then, are you sure? And based on their affirming the more rational rule,
     what might be some possible alternative solutions?
S: So based on the more rational belief, how then would you act; what could
     you then do to follow through? This could really be the missing key. They've
     had a lot of training in communication and stuff but I can see where there're
     still each insisting that their way is right and the other should act differently.
CH: Will you be seeing them prior to our next supervision session?
S: Yes, next Tuesday.
CH: I'd ask that you spend that session with them focusing entirely on Debate
     . . . without moving on to Enactment. This couple would seem to likely
     benefit by a more intense Debate process given the apparent lack of focus
     therein in their previous therapies. I have several structured interactional
     Debate activities that you might employ during the session to reinforce
     your verbal discussion.
S: OK.
CH: Why don't you summarize what your thinking is relative to what you exper-
     ienced in our supervision today and then we can look over those structured
     Debate activities . . .

CLOSING COMMENTS: GROUP AND SELF-SUPERVISION

REFT supervision is also commonly conducted within a group context. All that has been described throughout this chapter applies equally to the group context. Supervision in small groups of four to six supervisees, however, offers several additional advantages: (1) supervisees learn from the added interactions among themselves as well as with the supervisor; (2) the group can easily convert itself into a group therapy session offering the benefits of that context; or, it can also become a seminar to consider the potentials of shifting presuppositions or research issues; (3) alternatives in addressing procedural concerns can be more readily enacted in family "role play" within the group; and (4) following supervisory modeling relative to therapist distinctions, assessing family frames of reference, strategic change processes, and the like are also enacted more easily with "family members" present in the form of role play experiences.

Finally, one goal all REFT supervisory efforts have in common is to facilitate supervisees learning to supervise themselves. With the aid of video- or audiotaped sessions and a checklist of points to critique, experienced REFT therapists give themselves regular supervisory checkups. Items for such a checklist include: (1) How was the session actively structured? (2) If homework tasks had been previously agreed to, were they adequately reviewed? (3) How were family members' prioritized goals and accompanying objectives attended to? (4) What core irrational beliefs and rational counterparts were identified? (5) How were these debated? (6) Was there an adequate outcome to the Debate? (7) How meaningful was the Enactment for the family? (8) How was Feedback facilitated; were family members able to adequately self-affirm or reevaluate? (9) Is the therapist–family interaction too stylistic and patterned; if so, is it a helpful or problematic pattern that is present? (10) What homework assignments were agreed to and were they relevant to the session's content and process?

Encouraging supervisees to begin developing self-supervision standards for themselves such as the checklist criteria brainstormed above communicates the idea that supervision is a continual process throughout a therapist's professional career. By themselves, and when available and appropriate, in supervisee-supervisor or group contexts, they best persist at continuing the process to maintain the therapeutic sharpness and personal stamina to work with families.

EPILOGUE: The REFT Advantage

REFT, as was described in Chapter 3, has been offered here in this book as a new "clinical epistemology." As an essentially clinical rather than academic discipline, clinical epistemology is not intended to represent an evolving body of theory or research, but rather an evolving set of practical, clinical procedures. As a clinical epistemology, the REFT advantage is considerable.

Family systems, including those behaviors they label as "problems," do not behave on the basis of observable words, actions, and emotions alone, but always on the basis of these observable forms of human expression *plus* the beliefs they have about their own and others' behaviors. REFT is concerned with making this interaction and especially the contribution of family members' beliefs very plain. It explains particularly how certain types of beliefs (i.e., family members' evaluations) are crucial contributors to the existence and persistence of problems, as well as their alleviation.

While REFT presupposes the importance of beliefs in family therapy, it does not presuppose beliefs to be the only focus; effective and efficient family therapy is conceived as considering and dealing with a number of factors which are interrelated more systematically as opposed to hierarchically. REFT's ABCDEF alerts the therapeutic system to the primacy of process, thereby helping to escape the often bewildering array of content issues that present themselves. No matter the sophistication or accuracy of attention afforded to specific elements, if the attention given to the overall process falters, then all seemingly helpful interpretations and interventions are likely to be of limited benefit, especially over the longer term. Not only is the B element important, but equally so is assessing the A and C, and then actively engaging in D, E, and F. All are critical elements of the process.

This is the fundamental lesson of REFT and one, once adhered to, that provides clear strategic advantages. When the interactions of a family are in "rational" harmony both with individual family members' own designs for life and the normative requirements of the larger culture, then greater satisfaction and attainment of life goals are probable. REFT offers directions for traveling through the complex crossroads of family life disrupted by "problems." These directions offer a means of experiencing the excitement occasioned by effective and efficient family therapy efforts.

References

Ashby, W. R. (1956). *Introduction to cybernetics.* New York: Wiley.

Bateson, G. (1971). The cybernetics of "self": A theory of alcoholism. *Psychiatry, 34,* 1–18.

Bateson, G. (1972). *Steps to an ecology of mind.* New York: Ballantine.

Bateson, G. (1979). *Mind and nature: A necessary unit.* New York: Dutton.

Bateson, G., Jackson, D., Haley, J., & Weakland, J. (1956). Toward a theory of schizophrenia. *Behavioral Science, 2,* 154–161.

Beavers, W. R. (1977). *Psychotherapy and growth: A family systems perspective.* New York: Brunner/Mazel.

Beck, A. T., Rush, A. J., Shaw, B. F., & Emery, G. (1978). *Cognitive therapy of depression: A treatment manual.* (Unpublished.)

Bedford, S. *Instant replay: A method of counseling and talking to little (and other) people.* New York: Institute for Rational Living.

Bernard, M. E. (1981). Private thought in rational-emotive therapy. *Cognitive Therapy and Research, 5,* 125–143.

Bernard, M. E., & Joyce, M. R. (1984). *Rational-emotive therapy with children and adolescents: Theory, treatment strategies, preventive methods.* New York: Wiley.

Bodin, A. M. (1981). The interactional view: Family therapy approaches of the mental research institute. In A. S. Gurman & D. P. Kniskern (Eds.), *Handbook of family therapy,* (pp. 267–309). New York: Brunner/Mazel.

Boyd, J. D. (1978). *Counselor supervision.* Muncie, IN: Accelerated Development.

Chance, M. R. (1966) An interpretation of some antagonistic postures: The role of "cut off" acts and postures. *Symposium of the Zoological Society of London, 8,* 71–89.

de Shazer, S. (1985). *Keys to solution in brief therapy.* New York: Norton.

DiGiuseppe, R., & Zeeve, C. (1985). Marriage: Rational-emotive couples counseling. In A. Ellis & M. E. Bernard (Eds.), *Clinical applications of rational-emotive therapy,* (pp. 55–80). New York: Plenum.

Dolliver, R. H. (1979). The relationship of rational-emotive therapy to other psychotherapies. In A. Ellis & J. M. Whiteley (Eds.), *Theoretical and empirical foundations of rational-emotive therapy.* Monterey, CA: Brooks/Cole.

Dryden, W. (1984). *Rational-emotive therapy: Fundamentals and innovations.* London: Croom Helm.

Ellis, A. (1957). *How to live with a "neurotic."* New York: Crown.

Ellis, A. (1958). Rational psychotherapy. *Journal of General Psychology, 59,* 35–49.

Ellis, A. (1962). *Reason and emotion in psychotherapy.* Secaucus, NJ: Lyle Stuart.

Ellis, A. (1970). Rational-emotive Therapy. In L. Hersher (Ed.), *Four psychotherapies.* New York: Appleton-Century-Crofts.

Ellis, A. (1971). Emotional disturbance and its treatment in a nutshell. *Canadian Counselor, 5,* 168–171.

Ellis, A. (1973). *Humanistic psychotherapy: The rational-emotive approach.* New York: McGraw Hill.

Ellis, A. (1977). *How to live with—and without anger.* Secaucus, NJ: Citadel Press.

Ellis, A. (1978). Toward a theory of personality. In R. J. Corsini (Ed.), *Readings in current personality theories.* Itasca, IL: Peacock.

Ellis, A. (1979). The theory of rational-emotive therapy. In A. Ellis & J. M. Whiteley (Eds.), *Theoretical and empirical foundations of rational-emotive therapy,* (pp. 33–60). Monterey, CA: Brooks/Cole.

Ellis, A. (1980). Rational-emotive therapy and cognitive behavior therapy: Similiarities and differences. *Cognitive Therapy and Research, 4,* 325–340.

Ellis, A. (1982). Rational-emotive family therapy. In A. M. Horne & M. M. Ohlsen (Eds.), *Family counseling and therapy,* (pp. 302–328). Itasca, IL: Peacock.

Ellis, A. (1984). Rational-emotive therapy. In R. J. Corsini (Ed.), *Current psychotherapies,* (pp. 196–238). Itasca, IL: Peacock.

Ellis, A. (1987). The impossibility of achieving consistently good mental health. *American Psychologist, 42,* 364–375.

Ellis, A., & Becker, I. (1982). *A guide to personal happiness.* North Hollywood, CA: Wilshire Books.

Ellis, A., & Harper, R. A. (1975). *A new guide to rational living.* North Hollywood, CA: Wilshire Books.

Eschenroeder, C. (1982). How rational is rational-emotive therapy? A critical appraisal of its theoretical foundations and therapeutic methods. *Cognitive Therapy and Research, 6,* 274–282.

Fisch, R. Weakland, J., & Segal, L. (1982). *The tactics of change: Doing therapy briefly.* San Francisco: Jossey-Bass.

Fisch, R., Weakland, J., Watzlawick, P., Segal, L., Hoebel, F., & Deardorff, C. (1975). *Learning brief therapy: An introductory manual.* Palo Alto, CA: Mental Research Institute.

Genest, M., & Turk, D. C. (1981). Think-aloud approaches to cognitive assessement. In T. V. Merluzzi, C. R. Glass, & M. Genest (Eds.), *Cognitive assessment.* New York: Guilford.

Glansdorff, P., & Prigogine, I. (1971). *Thermodynamic theory of structure, stability, and fluctuations.* New York: Wiley.

Goldenberg, I., & Goldenberg, H. (1980). *Family therapy: An overview.* Monterey, CA: Brooks/Cole.

Greiger, R., & Boyd, J. (1980). *Rational-emotive therapy: A skills-based approach.* New York: Van Nostrand Reinhold.

Gurman, A. (Ed.) (1981). *Handbook of family therapy.* New York: Brunner/Mazel.

Haley, J. (1970). Family therapy. *International Journal of Psychiatry, 9,* 233–242.

Haley, J. (1976). *Problem-solving therapy.* San Francisco: Jossey-Bass.

Harris, R. (1977). Rational-emotive therapy: Simple but not easy. *Rational Living, 12,* 9–12.

Hauck, P. A. (1980). *Brief counseling with RET.* Philadelphia: Westminster Press.

Hoffman, L. (1981). *Foundations of family therapy.* New York: Basic Books.

Horney, K. (1942). *Self-analysis.* New York: Norton.

Howe, R., & von Foerster, H. (1974). Cybernetics at Illinois. *Forum, 6,* 15–17.

Jackson, D. (1965). Family rules: Marital quid pro quo. *Archives of General Psychiatry, 12,* 589–594.

Jackson, D. (1977). The study of the family. In P. Watzlawick & J. Weakland (Eds.), *The interactional view.* New York: Norton.

Keeney, B. P. (1983). *Aesthetics of change.* New York: Guilford.

Keeney, B. P., & Ross, J. M. (1983). Cybernetics of brief family therapy. *Journal of Marital and Family Therapy, 9,* 375–382.

Keeney, B. P., & Ross, J. M. (1985). *Mind in therapy: Constructing systemic family therapies.* New York: Basic Books.

Koestler, A. (1979). *Janus: A summing up.* New York: Vintage Books.

Maultsby, M. (1975). *Help yourself to happiness.* New York: Institute for Rational Living.

Maultsby, M., & Ellis, A. (1974). *Techniques for using rational-emotive imagery.* New York: Institute for Rational Living.

McKelvie, W. H. (1987). The MRI interactional view and Adlerian psychology: A comparison. In R. Sherman & D. Dinkmeyer (Eds.), *Systems of family therapy: An Adlerian integration,* (pp. 143–174). New York: Brunner/Mazel.

McPherson, S. R., Brackelmanns, W. E., & Newman, L. E. (1974). Stages in the family therapy of adolescents. *Family Process, 13,* 77–94.

Mead, M. (1968). Cybernetics of cybernetics. In H. von Foerster, H. Peterson, J. White, & J. Russell (Eds.), *Purposive systems.* New York: Spartan Books.

Meichenbaum, D. (1977). *Cognitive-behavior modification: An integrative approach.* New York: Plenum.

Minuchin, S. (1974). *Families and family therapy.* Cambridge, MA: Harvard University Press.

Minuchin, S., & Fishman, H. C. (1981). *Family therapy techniques.* Cambridge, MA: Harvard University Press.

Nichols, M. P. (1984). *Family therapy: Concepts and methods.* New York: Gardner Press.

Nichols, M. P. (1987). The individual in the system. *The Family Therapy Networker, 11*, 32–38.

Nichols, W. C., & Everett, C. A. (1986). *Systemic family therapy: An integrative approach.* New York: Guilford.

O'Hanlon, B., & Wilk, J. (1987). *Shifting contexts: The generation of effective psychotherapy.* New York: Guilford.

Pask, G. (1969). The meaning of cybernetics in the behavioral sciences. In R. J. Rose (Ed.), *Progress of cybernetics.* New York: Gordon & Breach.

Rapoport, A. (1968). Foreword. In W. Buckley (Ed.), *Modern systems research for the behavioral scientist,* (pp. xiii–xxii). Chicago: Aldine.

Schultz, S. J. (1984). *Family systems therapy: An integration.* New York: Jason Aronson.

Segal, L., & Kahn, J. (1986). Brief family therapy. *Individual Psychology: The journal of Adlerian theory, research & practice, 42,* 545–555.

Slater, P. (1974). *Earthwalk.* New York: Bantam Books.

Smith, D. (1982). Trends in counseling and psychotherapy. *American Psychologist, 37,* 802–809.

Spivack, G., Platt, J., & Shure, M. (1976). *The problem-solving approach to adjustment.* San Francisco: Jossey-Bass.

Steinglass, P. (1978). The conceptualization of marriage from a systems theory perspective. In T. J. Paolino & B. S. McCrady (Eds.), *Marriage and marital therapy,* (pp. 298–365). New York: Brunner/Mazel.

Umbarger, C. C. (1983). *Structural family therapy.* New York: Grune & Stratton.

Varela, F. (1979). *Principles of biological autonomy.* New York: North Holland.

von Foerster, H. (1973). Cybernetics of cybernetics (physiology of revolution). *The Cybernetician, 3,* 30–32.

Walen, S., DiGiuseppe, R., & Wessler, R. (1980). *A practitioner's guide to rational-emotive therapy.* New York: Oxford University Press.

Watzlawick, P., Beavin, J., & Jackson, D. (1967). *Pragmatics of human communication.* New York: Norton.

Watzlawick, P., & Weakland, J. (1977). *The interactional view.* New York: Norton.

Watzlawick, P., Weakland, J., & Fisch, R. (1974). *Change: Principles of problem formation and problem resolution.* New York: Norton.

Webster's new collegiate dictionary. (1976). Springfield, MA: G. & C. Merriam.

Wessler, R., & Wessler, R. (1980). *The principles and practice of rational-emotive therapy.* San Francisco: Jossey-Bass.

Whitaker, C. A. (1976). The hindrance of theory in clinical work. In P. J. Guerin (Ed.), *Family therapy: Theory and practice,* (pp. 154–164). New York: Gardner Press.

Whitehead, A. N., & Russell, B. (1910). *Principia mathematica* (2nd ed.). Cambridge: Cambridge University Press.

Wilder, C. (1979). The Palo Alto group: Difficulties and directions of the interactional view for human communication research. *Human Communication Research, 5,* 171–186.

Woullf, N. (1983). Involving the family in the treatment of the child: A model for rational-emotive therapists. In A. Ellis & M. E. Bernard (Eds.), *Rational-emotive approaches to the problems of childhood,* (pp. 367–386). New York: Plenum.

Young, H. (1974). *A rational counseling primer.* New York: Institute for Rational Living.

Young, H. (1983). Principles of assessment and methods of treatment with adolescents: Special considerations. In A. Ellis & M. E. Bernard (Eds.), *Rational-emotive approaches to the problems of childhood,* (pp. 89–108). New York: Plenum.

Index

Index